HEALING
WOUNDS
of SEXUAL
ADDICTION

EXPANDED AND UPDATED EDITION OF *FAITHFUL AND TRUE*

HEALING *the* WOUNDS *of* SEXUAL ADDICTION

DR. MARK R. LAASER

FOUNDER OF FAITHFUL AND TRUE MINISTRIES

■ ZONDERVAN®

ZONDERVAN.com/
AUTHORTRACKER
follow your favorite authors

ZONDERVAN

Library of Congress Cataloging-in-Publication Data

Laaser, Mark.
    Healing the wounds of sexual addiction / Mark Laaser ; foreword by Gary Smalley,
Patrick Carnes.
        p. cm.
    Rev. ed. of: Faithful & true. c1996.
    Includes bibliographical references.
    ISBN 978-0-310-25657-1
    1. Sex addicts—Religious life. 2. Sex addiction—Religious aspects—Christianity. 3.
Sex addicts—Rehabilitation. 4. Sex addiction—Treatment.
    I. Laaser, Mark R. Faithful & true. II. Title.
    BV4596.S42L32 2004
    241'.66—dc22   2004007056

Interior design by Beth Shagene

Printed in the United States of America

09 10 11 12 13 14 15 • 29 28 27 26 25 24 23 22 21 20 19 18 17 16 15 14 13 12

CONTENTS

FAITHFUL AND TRUE

Rarely have I read every page of a book. When I received a copy of this book, I read it cover to cover. I underlined and noted passages I wanted to remember and reread. This is the most marked-up book I own.

One of the things that attracted me is Mark Laaser's description of healthy and unhealthy families. Chapter 6 alone, in which the author traces the roots of sexual addiction in families, is worth the price of the book. Never before have husbands and wives needed a deeper commitment to healthy marriages and families. Mark has eloquently unraveled the mystery behind addictive behavior, and he has helped me to see that, when our relationships are not alive and growing, the temptation for various kinds of addictions is unleashed.

The author clearly and concisely defines what a healthy relationship is and isn't. He explains what to avoid in your marriage and family that would move you toward the unhealthy range of behavior, and what to maximize so you can move toward the healthier range.

Rarely have I called authors of books I have read. In fact, I've phoned only two authors in my life. Mark Laaser was one of them. When I finished reading his book, I called him up to compliment him. This is a book everyone needs to read.

GARY SMALLEY

THE SECRET SIN

The Christian church, both Protestant and Catholic, is experiencing tremendous turmoil in the area of sexuality. We have Christian leaders whose sexual behavior has become a problem of credibility for their ministries. They ask forgiveness only to become embroiled in sexual sins again and again. The media exposes their folly, and the sacred becomes the focus of our culture's wit and sarcasm.

The problem seems epidemic. We have a clergyman, a Roman Catholic priest, who has 163 counts of sexual misconduct with children. We have a bishop whose affair became a national scandal—only to find that the woman has been involved with a series of ministers. We have a denomination facing close to a billion dollars in out-of-court settlements for child sexual abuse. We have a clergyman, who preached national crusades against pornography, arrested for the production and distribution of child pornography.

The church membership also struggles. Some struggle with inhibited sexual desire. God's desire for their sexual lives remains elusive. The sexual compulsivity of others drives them to secret lives of shame and self-hatred because they cannot live up to their values. Both types probably suffer the aftereffects of sexual abuse, the memories of which reside in the shadowy fringes of their consciousness. They do not know what troubles them, and even incessant prayer does not take away the pain.

Worse, our entire culture is in sexual crisis. The problems between men and women were highlighted by the nomination of Clarence Thomas to the Supreme Court. That a whole nation could be so absorbed and conflicted about what is exploitive sexual behavior underlines our sexual pain and uncertainty.

But parents confront this every day. The average age of first intercourse in our country is 16.2 for girls and 15.9 for boys. The vast majority of students are sexual by the time they are high school seniors. Parents do not know what to do. They know how poorly the old prohibitions worked for them. Yet in their hearts they know how unprepared their children are for sexual activity. All of this is shadowed by the AIDS epidemic, which is transforming our culture. Nothing more clearly connects responsible behavior and sex than this disease. By 1993 over a million Americans were infected with the AIDS virus. And with that statistic we sense the emerging awareness of our sexual pain.

The gospel message endures because Christians learn to transform suffering into meaning. Now is the time to focus that healing power on our sexual lives. We have needed voices to witness what sexual grace can mean. Dr. Mark Laaser in this book has done that. *Faithful and True* is written from the heart, in the context of his own healing. It presents the best of what we know about the disease of sexual addiction, and challenges the Christian community to face the sexual realities around us. It is a risky book to read if you wish to avoid your sexual self.

Most important, this book places sex in a spiritual context. As alcoholics, compulsive gamblers, and other addicts have found, the path to recovery is spiritual. As many of us who work in health care have found, God does not think in compartments. The Spirit works with medicine and science if we are open to the Lord. Such is the nature of this powerful book. And so should the reading of it be.

PATRICK J. CARNES, PH.D.
NEW FREEDOM TREATMENT PROGRAMS
SCOTTSDALE, ARIZONA

ACKNOWLEDGMENTS

This book would not have been possible without the strength, help, and support of many people who had faith in me, and in the project, at times when I desperately needed encouragement.

The countless hours it took to write this book would not have been available without the sacrificial love and patience of my family. My wife, Deb, helped inspire this book in more ways than she knows. What I have written about intimacy, I practice with her. She models how to be vulnerable and share feelings. Much of what I "preach" is behavior she practices. Her encouragement gently prodded me into sharing some of my feelings for the first time. And her forgiveness has shown me that genuine forgiveness is possible.

Over the years, my children, Sarah, Jonathan, and Benjamin, have put up with a father who sits and stares blankly into a computer screen. Countless times they quieted their activities and entertained themselves so I could write. More than this, they expressed genuine interest in my work and often asked how it was going. It is a special grace on their part to put up with a father whose work in the field of sexual addiction comes out of his own experiences. As they grow in maturity and faith, my prayer is that the sins of their father will not be passed to them.

In 1987, Pat Carnes became my hero, a prophet pointing to the true path of healing. Since then he has become a colleague, friend, and sponsor of my writing.

Foremost among the many guides along my personal journey are two gifted counselors, Tom and Maureen Graves. Their ability to gently confront, create a safe place to discover my pain, and show me how to love myself are profound gifts. They have also modeled and taught me the recovery process for all addictions.

What can I say about all my friends in recovery whose companionship was an ever-present help in times of both trouble and joy? For professional reasons, these fellow travelers must remain nameless.

An author is often encouraged by other authors. Writing is more about discipline and less about inspiration than I once thought! I am indebted to Jennifer Schneider and Ralph Earle, authors who encouraged me to be disciplined.

Countless counselors, therapists, and doctors have responded constructively to the ideas in this book. Special thanks to John Lybarger, Ph.D., Eli Machen, and Nils Friberg, Ph.D. for their critiques.

Authors do not write books alone. Books are written and then rewritten with the help of editors whose efforts get little credit. Twice now, in 1991 and 2004, Sandy Vander Zicht has been a gentle editor. She took what was often lofty, fuzzy, or confusing, and helped me to make it more intelligible. Thanks to Sandy and to Zondervan for having faith in me.

THERE IS HOPE

Once there was a young pastor who became a full-time individual, marriage, and family counselor. He, his wife, and three children lived in a nice, suburban neighborhood. The family had many friends and liked where they lived.

In addition to counseling, this pastor was an interim preacher at a local church, taught a course at the local Christian college, and served on the school board. A popular communicator, he spoke for various groups and was frequently interviewed on radio and television. He also enjoyed volunteering at a hospice. All in all, this pastor was well liked and respected by his community, and many turned to him for support, advice, and encouragement.

However, this pastor was also a sex addict. He had masturbated excessively since college. In graduate school he began visiting X-rated bookstores and massage parlors—a habit that continued into his professional career. Although he was afraid he would be caught and publicly humiliated, he could not stop practicing his sexual addictions.

Needless to say, his marriage, which on the surface appeared loving and stable, was very troubled. He and his wife were so busy with family and careers they had little time for each other. Lacking skills in intimacy and believing his wife didn't really love him, the pastor thought himself justified in finding a woman who would.

When several hurting and vulnerable women in his counseling practice looked to him for help, he initiated sex with them. He confused sex
with love and believed he really cared for the women, never realizing
how much he was hurting them.

The pastor was tormented by self-doubt. He didn't like himself very
much, and he wondered how these women could be attracted to someone like him. Time and time again he vowed to end the affairs, and time
and time again he fell into sin.

Eventually, a colleague found out about one of the affairs, and the
pastor was fired from his counseling practice. Hurt and disappointed,
the colleague and several others confronted the pastor. One, a doctor
and recovering alcoholic, said to the pastor, "Your behaviors with sex
seem like mine with alcohol. You're out of control. Why don't you let
us find you some help?" The doctor hugged the pastor, for the doctor
knew the pain of uncontrollable behaviors.

Though shocked and afraid, the pastor was also tired of his double
life—tired enough not to resist the efforts to find him help. Several days
later he entered the sexual addiction unit at Golden Valley Health Center.

In the months that followed, this pastor discovered the pain and joy
of healing. It was a process filled with upsetting childhood memories,
guilt for his behavior, and anguish over the abuse he perpetrated on others. His addiction had cost him a great deal. He would never counsel or
preach from a pulpit again. Several of his clients sued him. Some looked
at him and his behaviors with hatred and disdain. But the process was
also filled with the joy of being honest, of a new life, and of restored
relationships with his wife and friends. He began to discover the peace
of healing and decided he wouldn't trade it for the world.

Saved at the age of sixteen and ordained ten years before he found
healing, this pastor always felt unworthy of God's forgiveness. Although
he was admired by others, he felt they would hate him if they knew the
truth. Only by embracing honesty and undertaking the transforming
journey away from sexual addiction did he truly come to know God,
redemption, and restoration.

Sex addicts, like the pastor, commit a secret sin. It is so sinful that
almost all are too ashamed to talk about it. Yet their sin, a profound violation of God's law, threatens our culture and the very core of the Christian church.

The secret sin of sexual addiction grows from seeds planted in childhood and symptoms may go undetected for years. In adolescence, the indicators of this disease may be confused with normal sexual development. In adulthood, the disease grows progressively worse. Ultimately, if untreated, its victims will die.

The secret sin is an addictive disease that has existed since the beginning of time, yet for centuries it has been misnamed, mistreated, ignored, or completely undiagnosed. Even though it has killed, humiliated, and wounded countless people, some still believe it doesn't exist. Those who suffer from sexual addiction have been laughed at, scorned, and persecuted. Too consumed by shame to ask for help, they have been confined to lives of loneliness and isolation. Only recently have we recognized the secret sin as a disease and offered treatment to its sufferers.

Christians are not exempt from this disease. Experts speculate up to 10 percent of the total Christian population in the United States is sexually addicted. If true, this means that in a congregation of 500 members, 50 are sex addicts. And this percentage may be increasing. In one study, two-thirds of all Christian men admitted to "struggling" with pornography. In another study, 40 percent of pastors surveyed confessed to looking at pornography. Although these findings do not indicate the respondents are fully addicted, it is tragic that the percentages of those interacting with pornography are far higher now than just a few years ago. This is due in large part to the availability of pornography on the Internet. Christians who struggle pray ceaselessly, read the Bible constantly, and consult countless pastors, but they still can't stop. Discouraged, many leave the church.

Sexual sin is not new news to the church. Voices among us have consistently protested this immorality and called for repentance. Yet sexual sin remains a difficult topic to talk about. When "one of us" commits a sexual sin, the rest of us are shocked and embarrassed by the apparent hypocrisy and massive failure of faith. In response, we turn inward to our own shame, fears, and confusion, and try to keep the situation as quiet as possible.

It is time to bring the problem of sexual sin into the arena of public discourse within the Christian community. The church can no longer ignore sexual addiction or pretend it exists only "out there," for it plagues both our families and our congregations. *Healing the Wounds of*

Sexual Addiction is my attempt to examine and address the issue of sexual addiction among Christians. We will expose these secret sins to the light of the gospel and our best psychological understanding.

You may think you don't know a sex addict. Sex addicts, however, do not fit the popular stereotypes. They are otherwise gentle and kind. They care deeply for others. To fellow church members they appear to be ideal Christians. But a secret side of them does evil and harmful things, sexual things, some of them too horrible to fully describe. Their sexual activity is uncontrollable and they can't stop. They are addicted.

But there is hope. In his classic book, *Out of the Shadows*, Dr. Patrick Carnes recognized that "out of control" sexual behavior resembles the behavior of alcoholics and that many people are addicted to sex. Carnes applied the same kind of treatment to sexual addiction that has been keeping alcoholics sober for fifty years. Because of the work of Carnes and others, thousands of sex addicts have stopped committing sexual sins. They are achieving "sexual sobriety," or what Christians might refer to as "sexual purity."

There is hope for the church and the many people in it who suffer secretly or publicly from sexual sin. There is hope for spouses, families, and friends. There is hope for countless thousands of people whose faith has been betrayed by the sexual sin of a pastor or other Christian leader. There is hope for the victims of sex addicts. There is even hope for those who long ago left the church when their sexual sin was met with judgment rather than help.

The story of the Samaritan woman in John 4 gives me hope. Married five times and currently living with a man who is not her husband, she is amazed when Jesus offers her—a sexual sinner—the living water of salvation. After Jesus heals her, he does not go into her village to preach to the respectable people—the adulterous woman does. Jesus entrusts the message of salvation to a redeemed sexual sinner. Talk about hope!

Finally, I know there is hope because I am recovering from sexual addiction. I no longer say I am a sex addict. Many characteristics describe me: committed Christian, husband, father, counselor, teacher, and writer. I am also the young pastor described at the beginning of this introduction. My sexual sins damaged many people, betrayed the trust of others, and brought painful consequences to me. Like the Samaritan woman, I too have stood at the well in the heat of the day, full of shame, lonely, afraid, and too proud to ask for help. God found me there. Through the help of many others, I am learning the peace of being in recovery. It is because of my own pain and desperation that I reach out to help others in theirs. I pray this book will show the way to the living water only God can offer.

TODAY THERE IS AN EVEN GREATER NEED FOR HOPE

It has been over a dozen years since I wrote the first edition of this book, *The Secret Sin*. Since it was first published, some things have changed and some have not. The realities Pat Carnes describes in his foreword are as true today as they were in 1992, perhaps more so. There is an escalating crisis in the church and in our culture. Some forms of sexual acting out are epidemic. Rarely does a week go by that I don't get a call about a "fallen" pastor or missionary. Today we are routinely exposed to sexual behaviors most would have considered aberrant just a decade ago. The availability of pornography through mainstream media has increased dramatically. Even "prime-time" television programs, once considered safe for family viewing, now regularly include sexually explicit content. We are waging a war on sexual addiction and sexual immorality—and we are losing.

One of the greatest problems we face today is the availability of sexually explicit material on the Internet. When this book was first published, the Internet was not yet widely used. Just a small percentage of the population even knew it existed. Today over 80 percent of us have surfed the Net at some time and the vast majority of us use it regularly. Pornographers, prostitutes, and sexual predators use it too, often in disturbingly creative ways. For example, just as the Internet was gaining popularity, pornographers purchased website domain names for many common terms and brand names—especially those likely to be used by children or adolescents, such as Cinderella and Coke. They used these names to create pornographic websites. As a result, whenever the word "Cinderella" was entered into an Internet search engine, pornographic material in the form of "pop-up" images appeared on the screen. This book now includes material that speaks to some of the unique problems posed by the Internet.

In addition to addressing recent Internet issues, this revision also includes the latest information about sexual addiction, as well as developments in my own thinking and learning. For example, I use the word *recovery* less, and the words *healing* and *transformation* more. We don't go backward and recover; rather, we go forward to heal and be transformed. I have also come to believe it is not helpful to describe families as healthy or unhealthy. Rather, it is better to see that all of us come from families who made mistakes. The important thing is to learn how we were wounded by those mistakes and how we can be healed.

Chapter 8 (formerly chapter 9), "The Journey of Healing," has been completely rewritten to include greater reliance on spiritual growth and biblical principles. The previous chapter included an extensive explanation of the Twelve Steps as a tool for healing. I continue to believe the Twelve Steps contain a great deal of spiritual wisdom and still encourage people to practice them and to attend meetings. However, I have come to believe the Twelve Steps do not emphasize enough the radical spiritual transformation that can only be achieved through a more intimate relationship with Jesus Christ. The new chapter still contains the wisdom of the Twelve Steps but teaches these principles within the larger context of biblical principles.

This book was written by a male sex addict and is obviously influenced by a male perspective. Some might think only men can be sexually addicted. However, this is not the case. Even the first edition of this book contained examples of female sex addicts. There is a dramatic rise in our awareness of the prevalence of female sexual addiction. For decades, our culture has encouraged women to be more aggressive and assertive. Some of this has been good. Women today have equal opportunities with men in many areas. However, just as men can use their power in unhealthy ways, so can women, and increasing numbers have become sexually addicted.

This revision is sensitive to the unique needs and issues of female sex addicts. Though more and more resources are being developed for women, it can be difficult for women to access that help because of the greater stigma attached to being a female sex addict. While a man who acts out sexually might be considered an "All-American Male," a woman is considered a "whore" or "slut" for the same behavior. It can also be problematic for women to participate in sexual addiction support groups attended mostly by men. However, because I believe male and female sex addicts have much more in common than they have differences, I have not included a special section on female addiction.[1]

Perhaps the most noticeable change is the addition of a new part four: "Healing the Wounds of the Church." This part is comprised of two chapters: "Sexually Addicted Pastors and Priests" (formerly chapter 5) and "Healing for Congregations." In recent years I have worked with an ever-growing number of churches whose pastors have "fallen." It seemed like a good time to address this problem by creating a section devoted to the unique needs of pastors and congregations.

God is good and gracious. I continue to heal and grow. I have been sober for seventeen years. Today, my wife, Debbie, and I work more and more as a team in ministering to others. Our marriage continues to transform into the one-flesh union God calls us to. Most of all, we believe with always increasing faith that true healing is possible. Our ongoing prayer is that this book will be a start for you on your own journey of healing.

PART I

WHAT IS SEXUAL ADDICTION?

CHAPTER 1

SEXUAL ADDICTION AND SIN

I recently talked with a pastor about the shame of being a sexually addicted Christian. By every indication this pastor is successful. He has developed a large church "full of many gifts of the Spirit." Well liked by his people, he preaches wonderful sermons. He is married, has children, and appears to be a normal family man.

Yet this pastor leads a double life. Many days he is drawn to a local park, where he meets men whose names he does not know and engages in sex with them. Most of these encounters last less than thirty minutes, and no words are spoken. He then returns to his office feeling emptier than before. Looking for intimacy, he finds instead only frustration and fear. When will someone from his church find out?

This pastor knows he is committing the sin of sodomy. He prays, fasts, reads Scripture, and yet he cannot stop. He is alone. Who can he tell? Disclosing this behavior would cost his job, family, career, and reputation.

SEXUAL ADDICTION AS A SIN

Sexual addiction is a sickness involving any type of uncontrollable sexual activity. Because the addict can't control his or her sexual behavior, negative consequences eventually result.

Whenever I speak to Christians about sexual addiction, someone always asks, "When you call these sexual behaviors an addiction or a disease, aren't you forgetting that they are sinful? People should repent, change their ways, and get right with God." I always agree with these statements. The sexual behaviors that become addictive are sinful. People should repent, change their ways, and get right with God. Repentance, behavior change, and a deeper relationship with God are all goals of the healing journey for a sex addict. I usually respond to this question with another question: How long do you expect repentance and change to take?

Sin and addiction have some common characteristics. Like an addiction, sin is uncontrollable and unmanageable. In fact, God had to sacrifice his only Son because we could not manage our own lives. Sexual addiction is about trying to control behaviors—and failing. Just like alcoholics, sex addicts tell themselves they can quit tomorrow if they want to. They like to think they are in control, but they are not. Indeed, their inability to give up the illusion of control is precisely what prevents sex addicts from healing. It is the same with any sin. Our attempts to control our lives prevent us from trusting God to care for us.

Addiction provides an escape from feelings. Despite experiences of God's love and power, people of faith sometimes have fearful, distrustful natures that drive them to seek an escape from feelings. Consider the prophet Elijah. After he defeated the priests of Baal on Mount Carmel, he was afraid for his life. Rather than face his fears, he ran away and hid in a cave. Jonah ran from his fears of God's preaching assignment and ended up in the belly of a whale. The disciples fled in fear from those who came to arrest Jesus in the Garden of Gethsemane. Just like an addiction, this drive to escape painful emotions is unmanageable. It is our inherited sin nature. Addictions provide a way of escape; a false solution; a means to control loneliness, anger, anxiety, and fear.

Addictions, being unmanageable, also lead to destructive consequences. Addictions destroy lives, break up families, ruin careers. Sin too has its consequences. Romans 6:23 tells us the wages of sin is death.

Most sex addicts experience devastating shame and believe they are totally worthless. In the Garden of Eden, before Adam and Eve sinned they were naked and unashamed. After sinning, however, they felt shame. Because we are sons and daughters of Adam and Eve, we also feel shame when we sin.

Therefore, a clearer understanding of addiction provides a deeper understanding of sin. Sin is more than just a list of immoral behaviors. Sin is the lack of a relationship with God and the destructive behaviors committed as a result. Sin is unmanageable and causes people to distrust God, to control their own lives, and to commit behaviors destructive to themselves and others. Sin causes shame and leads to death. Unmanageability, escape, shame, and—for some—addiction, are interwoven into the very fabric of sin.

SEXUAL ADDICTION AS A DISEASE

Sexual addiction is also a disease—a situation in which something normally healthy becomes unhealthy. Both sexual addiction and disease have observable symptoms and a natural progression that, if left untreated, get worse and eventually lead to death.

Defining sexual addiction as a disease is also consistent with a definition of sin. Sinfulness has a cause. We inherit original sin when we are born. And sin has symptoms. We don't trust God. We make unhealthy choices. We try to control our own lives. Like disease, sinfulness is a degenerative process. The Bible continually warns us that we can sink deeper and deeper into sin. Sinfulness can eventually kill us.

The concepts of addiction and disease clarify and deepen our understanding of the consequences of sin. In accepting that sexual addiction is a disease and a sin, we must also accept that the devil, the personification of evil, is at work in sexual addiction. He uses many devices to create sexual addiction, including unhealthy family dynamics, abuse, and feelings of shame. The devil convinces us we are evil and irredeemable. He sows hopelessness by convincing us we won't get well. There is no question in my mind that we are engaged in spiritual warfare when we attempt to heal sexual addiction.

"MORAL" SEXUAL SIN

Sexual addiction is a disease and it involves sinful behavior. It is not my purpose to provide a theological definition of what is sexually sinful.

Most immoral behaviors, such as infidelity or child abuse, are plainly sinful. However, there are sex addicts and sexual activities that, on the surface, appear moral.

Consider the example of the sex addict who never engages in sexual activity with anyone except his wife, yet uses sex with his spouse as an escape from intimacy, not as an expression of it. In this case, the sex addict treats his spouse simply as a body and not as a spirit. Here, sex, although it is with a spouse, is really no different than masturbating. In these situations, the same characteristics of addiction apply. Over time, the addict wants more and more and becomes bored and unfulfilled in the marital sexual relationship. On the surface, he is faithful. But God, looking at his heart, discerns his motives.

These sex addicts don't know how to be emotionally or spiritually intimate with a spouse and believe they will find intimacy in sexual contact. Using sex to mask their loneliness, they are unwittingly driven deeper into loneliness, never revealing their feelings. They might even say to themselves, "As long as I remain faithful to my spouse and as long as sex is good, I don't have a problem and our relationship is good." In fact, the relationship is not good, and the sexual activity becomes an addictive way to avoid the pain of the poor relationship.

Whether their sexual behavior is inside or outside of marriage, sex addicts are lonely and isolated. They use sex for all the wrong reasons. The question is not whether or not their sexual activity is considered moral. The question is whether or not sex is an expression of intimacy or an escape from it. One definition of sin suggests it is any activity that separates us from God and from others. By this definition, purely physical sexual activity in a marriage devoid of intimacy is perhaps addictive and could be considered sinful.

Sex addicts may have family and friends. They may be active leaders. However, no one really knows them. They haven't told anyone who they are, what they feel, and what they've done. Christian sex addicts think if they were really known by those around them, they would be hated, shunned, laughed at, or punished. A key question of this book, and one every believer needs to consider, is: Will Christians help to heal, or will they help to increase, this shame, loneliness, fear, and woundedness? Unfortunately, in too many cases we have "shot the wounded," rather than healed them.

SEXUAL ADDICTION VS. NORMAL SEXUALITY

I am frequently asked about the differences between sexual addiction and normal sexuality. This question is especially acute for adolescents, teens, and single adults. The distinction between sexual addiction and normal sexuality is not about experiencing sexual feelings, but how we express them. God created sexuality. He told Adam and Eve to be fruitful and multiply. By God's design, everyone has sexual attractions and longings. It's what we do with those attractions and longings that makes the difference.

Below is a simple chart that provides a brief overview of the differences between sex addicts and non-sex addicts.

Behaviors and Thoughts	Sex Addicts	Non-Sex Addicts
Thinks about sex	Constantly	Occasionally
Encounters sexual stimuli, such as pornography or an attractive person	Initiates a cycle of sexual thoughts and hoped-for sexual activities. Disregards all moral and spiritual boundaries.	Notes the stimulus and moves on to other thoughts. Considers all moral and spiritual boundaries.
Masturbation	Becomes a habitual pattern used to medicate feelings.	Experiments but doesn't allow it to become a pattern.
Experience of sexual sin	Goes through a cycle of guilt and shame but repeats the sin.	Repents, confesses, and learns from the experience.
Marital sexuality	Selfish use of spouse to meet needs, including the need to avoid feelings.	Selfless expression of the deepest levels of emotional and spiritual intimacy.

As you read the following chapters that explain sexual addiction and where it comes from, I encourage you to wrestle with this question: What is the purpose of sexuality? The answer will provide greater understanding of the differences between sexual addiction and normal sexuality.

CHAPTER 2

BUILDING-BLOCK BEHAVIORS
OF SEX ADDICTS

Fred is an accountant. Each day he sits behind his desk, crunching numbers. But he has more than arithmetic on his mind. Today, for example, he thinks of a pornographic magazine he picked up at a newsstand. He also spends some time thinking about his secretary, who has been particularly nice to him lately. He begins to fantasize about what it would be like to sleep with her.

Fred exhibits some of the building-block behaviors of a sex addict. By "building-block behaviors," I mean behaviors that form a foundation upon which other sexual behaviors are built. These behaviors may start very early in the life of the sex addict, even before the child has developed enough physically to experience orgasm. Because these behaviors develop so early and are so basic, they are the hardest forms of sexual addiction to recover from. Building-block behaviors include sexual fantasizing; the use of pornography in all of its forms, including the Internet; and masturbation.

Fred's story depicts the three building blocks of sexual addiction working together in a vicious cycle. For a sex addict, fantasy is created by a need to satisfy deep emotional and spiritual longings. At the same time, the addict perceives sex as the solution to the need for love, touch, nurture, and affirmation. Pornography escalates the intensity of the fantasy to higher and higher levels of lust. Masturbation is the physical expression of that lust and perhaps the only touching the addict receives. Fantasy, pornography, and masturbation constitute a vicious cycle. Fantasy is escalated by pornography. Pornography stimulates lust. Lust expresses itself in masturbation.

SEXUAL FANTASY

The cornerstone for the three building blocks is sexual fantasy—thinking about sex. Normal people think about sex, and fantasy is not unhealthy in itself. Sex addicts, however, think about sex almost constantly. While normal people might note an attractive person then move on with their activities, sex addicts do not move on. Instead, they wonder how they might obtain sex with that person or they imagine what sex with that person would be like.

Fantasy can involve remembering past sexual encounters, imagining new ones, or planning how to obtain them. Sex addicts do not need pornography to start fantasizing. Any person or event might trigger sexual thoughts. If beauty is in the eye of the beholder, for sex addicts so is sexual stimulation. A person does not need to be wearing something sexually provocative for a sex addict to start thinking sexually about them. Many nonsexual things can be pornographically stimulating to a sex addict. For example, consider one of my favorite television game shows, *The Price Is Right*. The models on the show are attractive but not nude or provocatively dressed. However, a sex addict might readily fantasize about one of them. When that happens, the show becomes pornography for the addict.

Fantasy might also involve preoccupation with certain types of people—their appearance, age, status, or personality—or with certain parts of the body. Every fantasy is different. Many sex addicts are completely ashamed of the activities they've thought about even if they haven't acted on them.

What is it about fantasy that is so addictive? Fantasy by itself can be exciting enough for the addict's body to produce adrenaline, which is stimulating and elevates mood. Fantasy fuels the neurochemicals that facilitate human sexual response in such a way that the response takes place even without any physical stimuli. Fantasy can produce chemicals called chatecholamines in the pleasure centers of the brain that positively alter mood and even have a narcotic-like effect. The addict then uses these effects to escape unpleasant emotions, to change negative feelings to positive feelings, and even to reduce stress. For example, many sex addicts fantasize when they go to bed to put themselves to sleep. Don't underestimate the power of fantasy. Given the chemical changes it creates in the brain, sex addicts are, in reality, drug addicts.

Fantasies can be the addict's attempt to heal loneliness, boredom, and unmet needs. By fantasizing, sex addicts are able to create idealized images of sexual partners whom they believe will meet their every unfulfilled need. Sex addicts are often angry that their needs were never met. Fantasy meets those needs in imaginary ways and thereby medicates the anger. The fantasy partner is all caring, all attractive, perfectly nurturing, and completely sexual. Some addicts even fantasize about the perfect partner while having sex with a real partner, thereby attempting to make that partner into a perfect person.

USE OF PORNOGRAPHY

The second building-block behavior of sexual addiction is pornography. We live in a time in which use of pornography is increasing dramatically. When I first became addicted to pornography there were very few magazines available that featured actual nudity. Movies and TV still adhered to conservative moral codes. Videos and DVDs weren't available. The Internet was thirty years away. Since that time, our cultural appetite for newer and more provocative forms of sexuality has grown, and every media outlet—television, radio, movies, advertising, magazines, and more—has rushed in to meet the demand. Our cultural appetite for sexuality has escalated in addictive ways and we are paying the price for it.

Defining Pornography

Defining pornography can be difficult. If we define *pornography* as anything that displays nudity, many works in art museums would be considered pornographic. At the same time, there are instances of pornography on television that display no nudity at all. For example, many of the so-called "reality" programs don't show explicit nudity (although some come close) but do show sexually suggestive or explicit sexual situations. Could this not be considered pornographic?

Most of us would probably agree that pornography is writing about or displaying in some medium (magazines, videos, television, movies, the Internet) nudity or sexual activity that excites sexual feelings. Christians might add that pornography excites unhealthy, immoral, and sinful sexual feelings.

Sex addicts can be sexually excited by a wide variety of written and visual stimuli. Magazines like *Playboy* (and worse), R- and X-rated movies and videos, television shows (especially late-night cable and satellite shows), books that describe sexual acts, and Internet pornography sites excite most people. They display sexuality in immoral and unhealthy ways and incite sinful sexual passions. On the other hand, a sex addict might be sexually excited by something no one else would find stimulating. The determining factor in what makes the stimulus pornographic is how a sex addict turns otherwise nonsexual material into sexual fantasy. If you are an addict, this means you must determine what is pornographic for you and not worry about what is pornographic for someone else. In order to find healing, it is vitally important to identify and understand your own fantasy triggers. Chapter 11 addresses this in depth. If you are in a relationship with an addict, please know it is the addict's responsibility to identify and avoid pornographic materials. It is not your responsibility to protect the addict from all things you think are pornographic.

Other sex addicts are attracted to deviant sexual activity, such as bestiality or violent sex. Perhaps the most tragic forms of pornography are those that use and abuse children. Since the development of the Internet, the availability of incredibly perverse sexual material has increased in astonishing ways. Many websites now offer menus of specialized activities. Sadly, one recent study revealed that there are over two million different children depicted in sexual ways on the Internet.

Some television shows, written materials, movies, and Internet sites don't actually display sexual activity but do promote inaccurate information about sex. Consider how some soap operas portray sexuality and relationships. From them we learn twisted ideas of commitment, intimacy, sexuality, friendship, and faithfulness. It is important to recognize that, especially for sex addicts, pornography is more than just the hardcore material the Supreme Court would identify as pornographic. It starts with inaccurate and subtle messages that promote false teaching about marriage, family life, relationships, romance, intimacy, and sexuality.

Pornography and the Internet

In recent years, I have been horrified at the rapid development of the Internet as the world's number one source of pornography. A variety of studies have found that two-thirds of all Christian men have visited Internet pornography sites and struggle with them. Studies also reveal that 40 percent of pastors use the Internet to view pornography, and one-third of those had looked at Internet pornography in the last thirty days. More and more women are also accessing Internet pornography.

The Internet has become a crisis for the Christian community. Every day people lose their jobs, are arrested for illegal activity, and many churches lose pastors because of involvement with Internet pornography. I have never seen sexual addiction take hold in a person's life as quickly as it can by using the Internet. Gary, for example, acquired a new computer and Internet access last Christmas. By February, he had spent over $100,000 on Internet pornography and maxed out his credit cards, several of which were newly acquired.

Several factors make the Internet a powerful and dangerous source of addiction. Psychologist Al Cooper has written extensively on Internet addiction. He describes three factors called the Triple-A Engine— Accessible, Affordable, and Anonymous.[1] The first A is that the Internet is so accessible. Anyone with access to a computer and a phone line can use the Internet. Many public places now have Internet access. Kids can access pornographic material on computers in their school or public libraries. Adults can get involved at work. An unpublished study revealed that at one Fortune 100 company, 60 percent of the time male employees spent on the computer was devoted to pornography. It used to be that a person had to go to less-than-desirable places to buy pornography. Today the worst filth can be accessed on the computer from the comfort of one's home or office.

The second A is that the Internet is so affordable. While most sites require users to purchase material, they also offer free pictures to get the viewer hooked. A person can literally spend days, weeks, and months looking at free material. Membership fees for most of these sites are relatively inexpensive. Perverse material that used to cost hundreds and thousands of dollars is now accessible for a fraction of the cost. After accessing the free and cheap material, however, addicts are drawn into incredibly expensive materials as their appetites increase.

The third A is that the Internet is anonymous—or it seems to be. Users can access pornography from the privacy of their homes on personal computers. No one watches or is aware of what they're doing. Those who might have been embarrassed to buy pornography in public places can now get it without having to go anywhere. Historically, women have been reluctant to purchase pornography in public places. However, the Internet has eliminated the inhibiting factor of public exposure. This may be one of the reasons an increasing number of women are becoming addicted to Internet pornography. The truth is, the Internet is anything but anonymous—many organizations routinely monitor Internet usage. Businesses, schools, and churches now have monitoring software that tracks Internet use, including every site a user accesses. The former director of the FBI once told me that his agency has access to online services that could trace virtually anyone's Internet use. The Internet is not anonymous at all.

The Internet is an example of a tool that can be used both constructively and destructively. At the same time that it enables communication, research, and relational connection, it also gives lonely and isolated people access to material that promotes destructive and addictive activity.

MASTURBATION

The third building block of sexual addiction is masturbation. This activity often begins in childhood, when children are naturally curious and explore their genital areas. Most people learn from this self-exploration and develop a healthy sense of their bodies. Sex addicts, however, become preoccupied with masturbation.

Addicts learn early that genital touching is pleasurable. As children, this may be the only pleasurable touching they receive. Some sex addicts are never touched in nurturing ways by parents, and touching themselves is their only source of physical nurture. It may be that the pleasurable feelings are the child's only escape from painful family chaos. One sex addict told me he was so good at secretly masturbating as a child, he could do it in the middle of the living room with lots of people around and no one noticed.

Masturbating can become so repetitive addicts actually injure themselves. An eighty-year-old pastor's wife was admitted to the hospital for surgical repair of lesions in her genital area. Her husband was physically unable to father children and became impotent. He refused to discuss this with her and, if she ever expressed feelings of loss or grief, he quoted Scripture to her. She masturbated daily for fifty years, and the abrasiveness of that activity created the lesions.

For some, masturbation is only an occasional experience used to escape feelings or give expression to fantasies. But for others, masturbation takes place daily. In one extreme case, I worked with a sex addict who masturbated twenty times a day. The compulsive need to masturbate can take so much time it causes addicts to lose valuable work, family, and social time.

A frequently asked question is whether or not masturbation is a sin. This can be a particularly distressing question for Christian single adults. Many Christians correctly note that masturbation is never mentioned in the Bible. However, to effectively address this issue, it is important to consider overarching biblical principles as well. For most, the physical act of masturbation follows sexual thoughts or fantasies. In Matthew 5, Jesus teaches that looking lustfully at another person is equivalent to committing adultery. The overarching biblical principle concerns lust and fantasy. In light of this, the real issue with masturbation is what a person thinks about. If a married person masturbates while thinking about someone other than a spouse, that is sinful. If a person masturbates to fantasies of a spouse but the activity is not based on connecting to the spouse spiritually and emotionally, that is also sinful. My challenge to those who ask whether or not masturbation is sinful is to ask in return, "Can you masturbate without thinking of something sinful?"[2] If the answer is no, then masturbation is something to avoid.

A VICIOUS CYCLE

The vicious cycle of fantasy, pornography, and masturbation may satisfy the physical need for sex, but it never satisfies the emotional and spiritual hunger deep in the soul. Addicts never learned to feed that hunger in healthy ways. Instead, they seek to gratify their needs in the easiest and most accessible ways. Sex at that moment allows the addict to escape and thereby cope temporarily with unwanted feelings. Over time, more and more sexual activity is needed to escape negative emotions. However, more and more sexual activity also creates more negative feelings.

This vicious cycle makes sexual addiction a degenerative process. It gets progressively worse. Some sex addicts can turn off or slow down their sexual activity for periods of time, but during the course of their lives, some kind of sexual activity will get worse. In alcoholism this is called the "tolerance factor." It takes ever-increasing amounts of the addictive substance to satisfy the habit.

In sexual addiction, this tolerance, along with many other factors, may lead the addict to more of the same sexual behavior or to other forms of sexual activity. The following chapter examines additional sexual behaviors sex addicts may engage in.

CHAPTER 3

TYPES OF
SEXUAL ADDICTION

Not every sex addict experiences the same form of sexual addiction. In the last chapter, for example, Fred was addicted to fantasy and pornography, and the pastor's wife was addicted to masturbation. While these are considered building-block behaviors, other behaviors common to many sex addicts do not begin as early but develop over time. Such behaviors may range from the seemingly normal sexual encounter with another consenting adult, to illegal and abusive behavior, such as rape or incest. The behaviors described here, particularly sexually abusive behaviors, reflect deeper levels of emotional pathology.

SEX WITH A CONSENTING PARTNER

Ruth has had sex with at least five hundred men. At any one time she has ongoing relationships with eight men, and on a given day she may have sex with three or four of them. At night she frequents bars to recruit new partners. Looking for the love she never found in her father, she escapes her depression through frequent sexual encounters.

Ruth is a sex addict who engages in frequent sex with many consenting partners. Other sex addicts may have only one affair every few years. Still other sex addicts have sex with only one partner and sex happens infrequently. This kind of sexual activity occurs between both heterosexuals and homosexuals.

Some Christians mistakenly equate sexual addiction with homosexuality. They think acting out in homosexual ways is equivalent to addiction. However, this is not the case. There are many homosexuals who are not addicted to sexual activity. Some live celibate or monogamous lives with a committed partner. The source of the confusion could be that many contributing factors leading to sexual addiction may also be factors that lead to homosexuality. There is very little research on this, but I offer two observations based on my experience. First, since addiction and homosexuality may share some causative factors, there could be a higher percentage of homosexuals who are sexually addicted. Second, homosexual men are more likely to be addicted than homosexual women.

Sexual addiction with a consenting partner can be placed along a continuum. At one end are those who have only one partner and engage in sex infrequently. At the other end are those who have many partners and engage in sex frequently. Between are varying numbers of partners and frequencies. The definition of sexual addiction does not depend on the number of partners but on why addicts practice the sexual behavior and whether they can stop the behavior. Therefore, even if a person has had only one affair, it could have been addictive if sex was used to escape feelings, was not an expression of intimacy between two people, and led to destructive consequences.

For some sex addicts the consenting partner is the spouse. Some married couples avoid talking to each other by engaging in multiple, daily sexual acts. A husband may ask his wife to perform sexual activities she doesn't like and is even repulsed by. Spousal consent to these activities may be a sign of sexual co-addiction (see pages 198–99 in chapter 12 for additional information on co-addiction).

CYBER-SEX

The growth of sexual relationships between consenting adults on the Internet is often referred to as cyber-sex.

Betty, a pastor's wife, told me that when she first started participating in Internet chat rooms, she became so engrossed in her online relationships she lost all track of time. She didn't know what month it was and could not recall what she had done with her family, at work, or at church. She experienced a virtual blackout. She was so intoxicated with fantasy, lust, and excitement that her mind went numb. Within the second month of online usage, she progressed from chat, to sexual chat, to phone sex, to actually meeting three men for sex.

George, a mild-mannered farmer, loved to play online games. He often asked for a female partner. Sometimes this led to casual chatting after the game, but other times it led to sexual talk and, in one instance, meeting a woman in person for sex.

Mary, a businesswoman, traveled to many cities for her job. Before she left on every trip she arranged to meet with men she found through online "connecting" services. When I met her, she was active in ongoing affairs with three men in three different cities.

These three true stories illustrate the prevalence of online sexual connecting. In each case, the people involved were otherwise socially inhibited. They would not have been comfortable meeting people in public. They would have been even less comfortable making sexual connections face-to-face. However, the relative ease of connecting anonymously through a computer ultimately gave them the courage to connect in person.

For some, online sexual connecting may never go beyond sex chatting, but for others it can progress to actual sexual experience. There has been an explosive increase in the number of services that connect people for sexual activity. One service advertises itself as an "adult friend finder." This is especially appealing because every addict struggles with loneliness. We all have deep desires to be in community, to belong, and to be included. The Internet gives shy and otherwise timid people a way to make relational connections. This doorway originally appeals to loneliness and legitimate desires for connection, but can easily progress to sexual activity and eventually to addiction.

PROSTITUTION

The use of prostitution is very common for many sex addicts. Because prostitution clients pay for sex as if it were a business transaction, they do not need to get involved with their partners like they might have to if they began an affair. Some addicts even justify prostitution by saying, "No one gets hurt."

Today we have massage parlors, escort services, and "modeling" agencies to go along with the traditional hookers on the street. For the right price, prostitutes will even come to a client's home. Adult bookstores and bars feature various forms of nude dancing, and often the dancers or models engage in prostitution.

One popular form of prostitution is actually legal and takes place over the telephone. Late-night television is peppered with commercials for numbers that enable callers to "discuss" various sexual activities. The ads appeal to both erotic and emotional needs by featuring attractive women who talk about loneliness, friendship, connection, and intimacy. Sex addicts spend small fortunes on prostitution, just like alcoholics who drink away their paychecks. At our hospital, we treat sex addicts who have spent thousands of dollars on these phone services.

Prostitution is increasingly available on the Internet via chat rooms, downloadable images and video, and other forms of "virtual reality." Many prostitutes who used to need a pimp, escort service, or massage parlor to find clients can now do so on their own using the Internet. Anyone can create a website and market illicit services online. The same Triple-A Engine that makes Internet pornography so powerful— accessible, affordable, anonymous—also makes online prostitution powerful.

Prostitution appeals to the fantasizing nature of the sex addict. In the movie *Pretty Woman*, for example, when the businessman portrayed by Richard Gere asks the prostitute portrayed by Julia Roberts what her name is, she replies, "What would you like it to be?" She knows many of her customers have elaborate fantasies about whom or what they want her to be. Prostitution reinforces the fantasizing mindset of the sex addict.

Sex addicts may experience more kindness and nurturing from a prostitute than anyone else. One sex addict loves to be treated like a baby by prostitutes. He gets powdered, diapered, and cooed over as if he were an infant. With sex addicts and prostitution, we are not just dealing with perverted adults looking to satisfy their lust. We are dealing with babies and young children in adult bodies who are looking for love in all the wrong places.

EXHIBITIONISM AND VOYEURISM

Exhibitionism and voyeurism are less common than other forms of sexual addiction, but still destructive. Both behaviors can be illegal and those who are caught may be arrested. The stereotypes of exhibitionism and voyeurism are the "flasher" in a raincoat or the "Peeping Tom" lurking outside a window. However, these addictions are complicated and express themselves in many ways.

Mary, for example, owned a transparent green blouse that left little to the imagination. She wore it to various bars, not so much to recruit new partners as to watch the reactions of men who saw her. Arousing them gave her a sense of control she never had when her father and brothers sexually molested her.

Jay loved to go into clothing stores with dressing rooms in the middle of the store. He took clothes in them he never intended to buy and left the door slightly open waiting for women to come by. He felt a rush of excitement when he saw the surprised looks on their faces. Jay was addicted to his fantasies of those looks and what they might mean. He was also addicted to the adrenaline rush.

Tom, another sex addict, also liked to frequent clothing stores. He loitered in sections that sold women's underwear pretending to buy something for his wife. Tom stationed himself close to the dressing rooms hoping to catch a glimpse of someone changing.

These are but a few of the endless and creative ways sex addicts might exhibit themselves. Browsing in lingerie departments, positioning oneself to get a look when someone bends over, or simply undressing someone with the eyes are forms of voyeurism.

In addition to physical exposure and voyeurism, a person can perform these activities emotionally. Some addicts tell sexual jokes to get a sexual high. Other addicts are turned on by hearing intimate details of sexual activity. Such addicts may in turn talk about their own sex lives, thereby exhibiting themselves emotionally. This form of sexual addiction is often found in the counseling and clergy professions, where it is easy to gain access to the intimate details of people's lives. Not only is this a violation of professional ethics, it can be extremely uncomfortable for the counselee.

INDECENT LIBERTIES

Indecent liberties occur when a person initiates physical contact with another person for sexual excitement. The other person has not agreed to the contact and may even be unaware it happened. Grabbing, pinching, tickling, rubbing up against, and other forms of contact in places such as elevators and grocery stores may constitute an indecent liberty. The word *groping* can apply to this kind of activity. Clinically, it is often referred to as *frateurism*. Even hugs as an expression of caring may have a sexual meaning to the sex addict.

A recent participant in one of our workshops referred to himself as the "hugging priest." He came to us only after several female members of his congregation complained to the bishop about how uncomfortable they felt with his hugs. Another workshop participant, a missionary, loved to get on crowded buses and rub up against women there. He often touched these women in sexual ways as well. Even the awareness that he might get slapped gave him a sense of excitement.

This form of sexual addiction reveals the deep needs we all have to touch and be touched. When the natural desire is confused with sexual lust, it can lead to this abusive behavior.

OBSCENE PHONE CALLS

Obscene phone calls aren't limited to talking dirty or breathing heavily on the phone. Rick, for example, was a pastor who called female members of his congregation to talk about church business, and masturbated to the sound of their voices. Another pastor randomly called women out of the phone book and tried to arrange meetings, some of which became sexual.

BESTIALITY

Bestiality, or sexual activity with animals, is another broad category and may involve a variety of acts. Bestiality is a problem in some rural cultures where it may even be perceived as a humorous adolescent rite of passage. However, bestiality is certainly not limited to rural areas, and there are pornographic materials devoted specifically to this behavior. For example, Larry was a New York City policeman who moonlit for a local veterinarian to satisfy his addiction to have sex with large dogs.

This kind of behavior is among the most disgusting and revolting. It shocks our sensibilities because we can't imagine how humans could allow themselves to become involved with animals. The abusive nature of this behavior is obvious. As repugnant as this behavior is, if we remember that the sex addict is searching for love, touch, and nurture, it becomes some-what easier to understand. Animals, like dogs for example, love to be touched, are always glad to see us coming, and always sad to see us go. Many of us understand how important pets can be in the lives of other-wise lonely people. Bestiality is yet another example of how legitimate desires become destructive when they are confused with sexuality.

RAPE, INCEST, AND CHILD MOLESTATION

Some sexual activities are clearly exploitative, abusive, and criminal. Rape, incest, and child molestation are three. Rape occurs when phys-ical force is used to engage a person in sex against his or her will. Incest is sexual activity between members of a biological family. Child molesta-tion is an adult engaging in sex with a child who is dependent on that adult for care, supervision, or instruction. The adult may use physical force, even if this is limited to the size differential between the adult and the child. The adult may also use emotional force, the authority of the role the adult has in that child's life. These forms of sexual activity have serious legal consequences and generally involve prison sentences.

The term *pedophile* is often used to describe an adult who is sexually attracted to children under the age of twelve. Not all pedophiles are sex addicts and not all sex addicts who act out with children are pedophiles. Pedophiles may not act on their pathological orientation in addictive ways. Sex addicts who act out with children may not be primarily ori-ented to children. Many people who act out with children are repeat-ing experiences they themselves had as children. In fact, most sex addicts are victims of childhood sexual abuse (see chapter 5 for more information about the connection between childhood abuse and sexual addiction). Now that they are adults, they can be in control. This gives them a misguided sense that they have reversed the pain of what happened to them.

It may also be that adults who offend in this way repeat their childhood abuse because it reconnects them to the first time their sexual awareness was aroused. This is called *imprinting*. When adults continue to act out what was imprinted on them as children, they may be returning to their original feelings of sexual excitement. The concept of imprinting is an important one for anyone who works with adolescents and teens. Having sexual experiences before marriage has potent and long-lasting effects. One's first sexual experience is very powerful and should be reserved for marriage. When this kind of repetition occurs, it perpetuates the cycle of sexual abuse.

In addition to rape, incest, and child molestation, abuse of authority is another exploitive and criminal sexual activity. This includes sexual activity between two adults not biologically related, when one of them is in a position of greater power or authority, such as a doctor, lawyer, teacher, employer, or older adult. This is sometimes referred to as "authority rape." Although the person not in power may have consented to or even initiated the sexual activity, the consent or the initiation is not freely given because the situation is inequitable when one person has greater influence or emotional power over the other. In these situations the person not in power is the victim.

Authority rape assumes that the victim believes the exploiter to be powerful, knowledgeable, or even "sacred." The victim wants to be part of that power, to be nurtured by the authority figure, and does anything to secure this nurturance. The victim may have been molested as a child, and now associates sexual activity with nurture. In such cases, the victim projects parent-like qualities to the powerful person.

Some of these criminal forms of activity may reflect sexual addiction and some may not.[1] Some sex offenders are sociopaths (they have no sense of right and wrong), and/or they have other personality disorders. For them, acting out sexually may be expressions of these disorders, of anger and rage, or of a need to punish and control.

This chapter explored a number of activities a sex addict may engage in; however, this list is by no means complete. I chose not to describe some extreme behaviors.

The most common behaviors are still the building-block behaviors of fantasy, pornography, and masturbation, and some addicts focus on these activities alone. Others who commit more serious forms of sexual addiction may also practice these basic addictive behaviors as a way of controlling the more severe behaviors.

In diagnosing sexual addiction it is important to consider more than the behaviors alone. It's easy to be distracted by the immoral, illegal, or bizarre nature of some of them. Sex addicts may excuse their addiction to fantasy or pornography by saying, "I've never raped anyone, so I'm not a sex addict." However, if this person engages in any uncontrollable, repetitive sexual behavior, he or she is a sex addict.

Whether sex addicts have committed rape or only fantasized about sex, they have certain traits common to all sex addicts. The next chapter describes these common characteristics.

CHAPTER 4

UNDERSTANDING AND IDENTIFYING THE CHARACTERISTICS OF SEXUAL ADDICTION

Ryan is a successful doctor and respected family man. His bedside manner is quick and brusque, but he smiles often and says the right things. A popular man, he has countless friends. But Ryan and his wife generally don't have time for each other, being too distracted by their work, social life, and children.

Lately, after busy days at the hospital, Ryan has been engaging in sex with prostitutes. He also suffers from occasional outbursts of anger at work, but the staff excuses his behavior, saying he is a busy man and the stress of caring for his patients must be great. Everyone around him assumes that since Ryan helps others with their problems, he doesn't have problems himself. They also assume that since people around Ryan like him, Ryan must like himself. But Ryan hates himself, his behaviors, and his work. Being a doctor helps him feel important temporarily, but the feeling wears off. He is beginning to consider suicide.

Fortunately, as strange as it may sound, the chief of staff at Ryan's hospital intervenes. A hospital nurse driving home had witnessed Ryan picking up a prostitute. Ryan is let go from the hospital, but offered the opportunity to seek treatment for his problem.

Ryan's story illustrates several characteristics of sexual addiction. It also reflects the cycle of behaviors sex addicts get involved in and the possible consequences that can result. This chapter reviews the characteristics, symptoms, cycle, and consequences of sexual addiction.

CHARACTERISTICS OF SEXUAL ADDICTION

Poor Self-Image

Sex addicts like Ryan have a poor self-image. They perceive themselves as bad, evil people. Those around them may not know this, however, because sex addicts can act with bravado, be boastful, promote themselves, or appear self-righteous. They may also seem conceited or obnoxious. Sex addicts who try to convince others of how wonderful they are, are actually trying to convince themselves that they are good people.

Some sex addicts play a martyr role. Their perception that they are bad leads them to believe that the world and everyone in it doesn't like them and that bad things will always happen. They may feel everyone is trying to take advantage of them, and the only attention they can get is sympathy from those who feel sorry for them. Their behavior is extremely frustrating to relatives and friends because they are never happy, won't take or implement constructive advice, and continue to complain even in the face of apparent success.

Other sex addicts compensate for poor self-image by overachieving. They think if they receive praise for their achievements, they will feel better about themselves. However, whatever they might accomplish in life is never good enough to convince them that they are good people. Always looking for the next triumph or accomplishment, they become addicted to the high of winning. Some sexually addicted pastors are addicted to praise and admiration. But the temporary fix of being complimented on a sermon doesn't last long. By Sunday afternoon the old convictions of innate badness return.

Still others may be underachievers, never quite living up to their potential. They believe they will never amount to anything and are afraid to risk trying for fear of failure. They would rather live with the possibility they could accomplish something if they did try. "If I had wanted to I could have gone to law school and become a lawyer, but it just didn't work out," they may say.

Sex addicts may seem very self-sufficient. A basic belief is that no one will take care of them because no one loves them as they are. At other times or to other people they may seem very needy, as if they always depend on someone else to take care of them.

The negative self-image of the sex addict leads to chronic depression. The vast majority—71 percent, according to Patrick Carnes's research—has thought of suicide.[1] Many have tried; some have been successful.

Mood Alteration and Escape

Barry has a hard time sleeping at night. His job is stressful. His children are rebellious. He worries about money, and he and his wife argue continually about the checkbook and the charge cards. He frequently sneaks off to the bathroom, at home and at work, to masturbate. Now it seems he can't go to sleep without sex. Since his wife is unwilling most of the time, he either fantasizes or masturbates.

Very early in the life of most sex addicts, sex became a solution to painful situations. The pleasurable feelings of sexuality were perhaps the only relief they knew. Sex became an escape, a way of altering their mood. They felt no one else was doing anything for them, so they took matters into their own hands. Sex was a way of coping.

As sex addicts grow up, sex remains a means of coping with stress. When painful feelings occur, sex becomes a way to medicate that pain. Even fantasy, without a more direct form of sexual contact, can be soothing to a sex addict.

Sense of Entitlement

When there isn't stress, sex can also be seen as a reward. Since sex addicts believe no one will take care of them and they must do everything for themselves, they begin to build up resentment. While one part of them feels they don't deserve anything and that they are bad people, a deeper and unconscious part of them wants to believe differently. Perhaps this is their spiritual side, the knowledge of their potential for goodness, a connection to a God who loves them.

Sex addicts, however, don't have a healthy sense of how to reward themselves or how to give themselves affirmation. Their anger and resentment are expressed as a sense of entitlement. "I deserve something," they reason. After surviving stressful events, performing well, or doing a good job, sex addicts may believe they deserve to be rewarded sexually.

Perhaps, for example, a sex addict is surviving a bad marriage or a bad job. They stay with it believing this is the moral and faithful thing to do. However, they also develop the feeling that they need to reward themselves to survive, and this medicates their feelings of loneliness and isolation. Sex becomes their reward. A sense of entitlement gives sex addicts the belief that they are justified in their sexual behaviors.

Unmanageability and Efforts to Control

A psychiatrist in South Carolina told me of a patient who was addicted to pornography. This person was a very religious man who read the Bible continually. He tried various methods to stop the pornography addiction, but without success. Finally, he took seriously a biblical injunction and plucked out both eyes because they continued to offend him. This story is a good example of how desperate addicts become in their efforts to control sexual behaviors, and of how unmanageable these efforts are.

Sex addicts try to stop but can't. They make promises to themselves and employ a variety of strategies to stop the behavior, much like an alcoholic. Some even injure their genitals or other body parts as a way to prevent their behaviors. Some turn rigidly and desperately to religion to stop their behavior. One man was baptized in four different churches in an attempt to take away his sexual desire.

Usually this religious approach leads to frustration, shame, and despair. A sex addict believes, "I was bad before. Not even faith can save me; therefore, I must really be a bad person." Often these people turn away from religion altogether. Going to church reminds them of their failure, or they feel God has not loved them enough to take away their lust.

When sex addicts try desperately to control their disease, they may succeed for various lengths of time. We call this "acting in," "white knuckling," and more recently "sexual anorexia." Acting in is the opposite of acting out. This is an extremely significant phenomenon. Many sex addicts deny they are addicted because they have been acting in or white knuckling for long periods of time. In this form of total self-denial they completely turn off their sexuality. Some married sex addicts may act out with themselves or others but not engage in sexuality with their spouse. In my current counseling practice, there are four men who look at pornography and masturbate but who will not engage in sex with their wives.

If we believe sex is sacred and a very normal experience between husbands and wives, sexual anorexia is not acceptable. It is denying a spouse the God-given gift of sexuality. It might be tempting to believe that those who don't engage in sex at all are living a righteous and pure life. This kind of thinking is based on a misguided belief that the more you deny the body the more spiritual you are. This is inconsistent with the teaching of both the Old and New Testaments. In the Old Testament, the Song of Songs is a virtual celebration of sexual union between a husband and wife. In the New Testament, the apostle Paul teaches beginning in 1 Corinthians 7:3 that husbands and wives should not deny each other sexually.

Acting in may be based on the Christian's fear of God. It is certainly biblical that we fear God in the same sense we fear parents who love us. We acknowledge their authority and know that, in love, they will punish us if needed to get us back on the right path. Although we may not understand it at the time, punishment is for our correction and rehabilitation. Proverbs 12:1 says, "To learn, you must love discipline; it is stupid to hate correction."

Christian sex addicts may fear God but not because they believe in God's loving correction. They are simply afraid. Acting in may be their way of manipulating God so he will not punish them. They turn off sexual feelings not to honor God out of healthy fear, but out of an unhealthy fear that God is an angry God.

This phenomenon has many parallels with eating disorders (see figure 1 on the next page). Anorexics act in, refusing to eat in an effort to control their weight, body image, and even their sexuality.

This is important for Christians to understand because at times sexual anorexics use Christian beliefs to justify their acting in. They mistakenly separate spirit and body in the belief that the body is innately bad. They reason that if the spirit can be "freed" from the desires and temptations of the body, a person will be more acceptable to God.

	Eating Disorder	
Overeating	**Nutrition**	**No eating**
Bulimia	Normal eating	Anorexia
Acting out	Healthy sexuality	Sexual Anorexia
Sexual Bulimia	Intimacy	"White knuckling"
		No sex
	Sexual Addiction	

Figure 1: Comparison of Sexual Addiction to Eating Disorders

Sexual self-denial is seen as highly spiritual behavior. However, Christians must remember that the Bible describes the body as "fearfully and wonderfully made" (Psalm 139), and treating it as inherently evil is to deny that we are made in God's own image.

Sex addicts make repeated efforts to turn off their sexual behaviors. Some may try moving, thinking they won't act out in a new environment. Churches often transfer pastors who have sexually acted out, thinking they will not repeat their behaviors because the shame of being found out once again would be too painful. However, this "geographic cure" rarely works. Because sex addicts don't know how to cope with shame and emotional pain in healthy ways, they use sex to cope.

Sex addicts sometimes try to get help by telling someone, but tragically they aren't believed, heard, or understood. Pastors may be quick to forgive behaviors or quick to moralize about the need to stop. Psychiatrists and counselors may excuse the sexual behaviors as normal. Because many therapists want to loosen rigid moral attitudes about sex and increase awareness of the joy of sex, they fail to hear the pain of sex addicts trying to explain that their sexual activity is uncontrollable. Sex addicts, often ignored or misunderstood by family, now face the pain of being ignored by the professionals they have turned to for help.

Denial and Delusions

Some sex addicts have never tried to get help, or else have stopped trying. Fear of strong moral judgment or social consequences keeps them silent and alone. They think, "Whom do I tell? Other people will get angry with me, reject me, or go running and screaming out of the room. I will lose my job, my family, my social standing." These fears create a deep need to be silent and an even more desperate need to control the behavior. This fear of negative consequences and rejection, and the resulting need to control, becomes intense for any addict. If they are ever confronted with their behaviors, they will either deny those behaviors or claim they are in control: "If I wanted to, I could quit."

Often addicts try to justify their behaviors. "I was lonely. My spouse is never sexual with me. People are always taking advantage of me. He seduced me in a weak moment." At other times addicts lie. "I really didn't do that. Where did you get that information? You are wrong. Are you trying to hurt me?"

One of the tools of denial is delusion, the belief that the addictive behavior is not really that bad or harmful. It is hard for an outsider to imagine how convincing sex addicts can be to themselves. We might wonder how a person could commit sinful, immoral, and illegal behaviors. The answer is that they may have deluded themselves into thinking their behaviors aren't that bad, and that they really aren't hurting themselves or anyone else.

People who are in denial or deluded may very well benefit from being confronted with their behaviors. Some may also need to suffer the consequences of their behavior in order to understand their negative and destructive nature.

Tolerance

The alcoholic builds tolerance of alcohol and therefore needs more and more alcohol to achieve the same mood-altering effect. A sex addict is no different, needing to act out more and more frequently to obtain the same high.

Terry frequented relatively safe gay bars in respectable neighborhoods. He made anonymous contacts with men who were gentle like him. This routine became boring, so he began to visit unsafe neighborhoods, where he found rougher men. These encounters became more physically dangerous. While he was afraid of this, it also excited him.

Part of the addictive quality of sex is that it is exciting, sometimes because it is dangerous. When an activity becomes routine, a sex addict may progress to more dangerous or exciting forms of it. This can be as simple as progressing from masturbating in private to masturbating in more public places, from having affairs with single people to having affairs with married people, or from picking up partners in relatively safe places to finding them in more dangerous places. For some, it may also mean progression to illegal forms of sex such as those described in the previous chapter.

Blackouts

Kevin met a man at a bar. Even though he had wanted to watch the World Series at the bar, he went home with this man and engaged in sex with him. Later that evening when he left, he was surprised to hear sirens and see crowds of people on the street. Many lights were out, and chaos reigned. While he had been having sex, San Francisco had experienced one of its most devastating earthquakes, yet he had not felt even the most violent of the tremors. Kevin is a good example of how powerful blackouts can be. The state of numbness, and what is clinically called "dissociation," means a person is literally unaware of even the most violent realities.

Alcohol often causes blackouts—the inability to remember what happened. Alcoholics can wake up in unfamiliar places and not know how they got there or what happened the night before. Sex addicts also experience blackouts when they are intensely involved in what they are doing. They too will wake up in strange beds and not know how they got there.

Blackouts occur for several reasons. Many sex addicts use alcohol, and that causes the blackout. Sometimes the experiences are so emotionally painful, the sex addict's brain naturally and protectively suppresses the memories. Or denial and delusional mechanisms are so strong the addict may "refuse" to remember.

Rigidity and Blaming

Phil, a seminary student studying to be a priest, struggled with masturbation and homosexual attractions. His spiritual director advised him that whenever he felt sexual temptation he should say the rosary five times and the temptation would go away. But it didn't work. He searched for other prayers and rituals that might help, but nothing did.

Phil's first ministry assignment was a conservative, ethnic parish in a poor neighborhood. The men there told jokes about homosexual men, and Phil joined in to avoid revealing his own sexual orientation. One night these men began ridiculing and taunting a man who seemed to them to be gay. Then they blamed homosexuals for all the problems in the world. While Phil disagreed with much of what they said, he too found himself getting angry and critical of the gay community. It is a common psychological dynamic to blame others for problems one experiences oneself. It is easier to be angry with others than with oneself. Phil was afraid of his homosexual feelings and found it easier to go along with the crowd than to honestly face his problems. His religious rituals had failed and he felt very lonely and isolated.

One result of sex addicts' desperate attempts to stop is that, like Phil, they may look for formulas to follow. They assume there is a right way and a wrong way to do things. If they could just get the formula right, then their sexual acting out would stop. This black-and-white thinking leads to rigidity. Addicts think there are good people and bad people, good groups and bad groups, and they desperately want to belong to the right side. In the search for the right people and the right side, an addict may become prejudiced against others who don't belong to this group. This leads to anger against those on the "outside." "If it weren't for them, things would be right with me and the world." This is a form of self-righteousness.

Self-righteousness leads to blaming. If there is a right way of doing things, there must also be a wrong way. Other people, institutions, or events may represent the wrong way and therefore are held responsible for the bad things that happen. "It is all their fault," a sex addict might say. "If he (or she) hadn't seduced me, I wouldn't have had the affair."

Sex addicts often look to the right religious group to take away their lusts. The man who was baptized four times felt he never did find the right church. If he had, one of those baptisms would have worked and his lust would have been removed. Some Christian addicts believe God will magically transform them into people who never experience sexual temptation. The theological correction to this misguided hope is very basic. If God did remove all of the temptations out there in the world, he would in effect be taking away our free will. The Bible is also consistent in teaching that temptations are opportunities to make moral choices and, when we do, we become stronger. James says, "Consider it pure joy ... whenever you face trials of many kinds, because you know that the testing of your faith develops perseverance" (James 1:2–3).

Codependency

Pat was addicted to going to massage parlors. At first he sought encounters with young and very attractive women. Gradually, he started seeking prostitutes who were older, resembling his mother. He also started to realize he wasn't so much interested in the orgasm as he was in the touching. Pat was looking for a mother. Every time he came out of the massage parlor he felt frustrated and cheated, but he kept going back, always looking.

Judy was raised in a very strict Christian home. While her father was occasionally home, he worked a lot, attended many church meetings, and had little time for Judy. He was strict, often angry, and very critical with her. As she grew up, Judy found herself getting attached to one man after another. She desperately needed their approval. She would do anything for them. If this included sex, so be it. Gradually, she found that she needed sex just to feel relaxed or temporarily content. Each man got bored with the relationship and left her. Every time, after intense grieving, she went out and found another. She has been married five times and has had numerous affairs.

These two cases illustrate that Pat and Judy were not only sex addicts, they were also codependents. They were looking for love and nurture and thought they could only find it in other people. The term *codependency* was originally used to refer to those who lived with and tolerated alcoholics. They were dependent on the alcoholic and therefore codependent on alcohol. Since that time, the field of codependency has come to recognize the anxiety of codependents and their desperate need for love and approval. This is the kind of need that enables them to tolerate addictive and dysfunctional behavior. It also motivates them to do anything to maintain that love and nurture. A codependent's anxiety forces them into either self-sacrificing behavior or into controlling behavior. In either strategy, they try to manipulate the love and approval of someone they depend on. Codependents are deathly afraid that a person will leave them. Our research with sex addicts has found that at a deep emotional level, they too are codependents.

Sex addicts crave the nurturing they have not received. They don't feel worthy of nurturance, but they seek it to fill deep holes in themselves. In looking for this connection, they become attached to people who represent this connection and can become totally dependent on them. Codependency affects how sex addicts relate to all people. They sacrifice themselves, their interests, and values in order to please someone else.

Relational Difficulties

Sexual addiction is an intimacy disorder. Sex addicts are not able to be emotionally vulnerable with other people. They would never tell anyone how they're honestly feeling, for they are probably not aware of how they feel themselves. Generally, their feelings are painful and to be avoided at all costs.

Sex addicts have great difficulty relating on a deep, personal level with other people. They may lie to cover up their behaviors, delude themselves and others about themselves, and generally lead a double life—one life everyone knows and the secret life only they know. These factors do not create meaningful relationships. The people sex addicts are most afraid of losing are the ones sex addicts are least likely to tell who they really are. They fear that if their loved ones really knew them, they would be rejected and abandoned.

One feature of the double life of sex addicts is their ability to tell some of their feelings to strangers yet not be able to talk at all to those close to them. This creates considerable anger for spouses, family members, and others who would like to get closer, can't, and then see their sex addicts opening up to others. But the sex addicts are less afraid of losing the stranger.

The relationships of sex addicts are often stormy and unsuccessful. They may be of a short-term nature and are certainly superficial, even though the sex addict may be very dependent on the partner. This dynamic of codependency is often called "enmeshment." A sex addict may desperately cling to someone for love, attention, and approval: "I would die if you left me."

Enmeshment can be dramatic, but it is not deeply intimate. Sex addicts may be enmeshed with people who need them desperately, allowing them to feel needed. Or they may be enmeshed with people who take care of them, thus allowing them to be irresponsible.

As part of their secret, double lives, sex addicts do not like being responsible for their time. They lie about where they've been and whom they've seen. They love free time and jobs that don't have regular structure, because it gives them the freedom to escape to their addictive activities. They also spend money on themselves and their addictive activity and don't like having to explain where it went. Sex addicts may also be compulsive spenders for things other than sexual activities.

Sex addicts are "slippery." They have lots of acquaintances but no friends. They may be the life of the party but no one knows them. They might have wonderful reputations, but it would shock many to know what they do sexually. They avoid accountability to anyone so they have the freedom to pursue their addictive lifestyle.

Many sex addicts experience what is called "gender hatred," seeming to hate all men or all women. Men who sexually act out with women, for example, may be accused of hating women, particularly if the sex is exploitative, abusive, or manipulative. However, sex addicts do not actually hate all men or all women. Rather, they blame women or men for abuse suffered in childhood. If a man abused someone early in life, any man who later comes along may take on the attributes of the original abuser. The anger felt toward the original abuser is misplaced onto the current person in a process called "projection." Old feelings from previous relationships are projected onto new people and new relationships.

Sexual Ignorance and Confusion

Despite the fact that sex addicts have lots of sexual experiences, they may not know very much about sex. In fact, they may be full of misinformation or lack information entirely. Sex addicts typically grow up in families where sex is rarely discussed. If sex was discussed in their homes, the brief conversations almost always comprised negative messages full of the dangers of sexual immorality. The positive, healthy, and spiritual side of sex was never presented. Combine this negative teaching with the lack of positive teaching and an undercurrent of tension develops around sexuality. Sex is "forbidden." They were left to discover what they could from their own experiences, including pornography, or from misguided and immoral cultural teaching.

Forbidden sex elicits curiosity and excitement, a natural and adrenaline-filled "pull" that many of us feel toward anything we know little about. In adolescence, as sexual feelings naturally develop, anyone can become frightened of sensations that are in fact normal. Given our cultural fascination with sexuality, this can be a very confusing time.

If sex addicts were sexually abused as children by a parent or other family member, the most significant connection with that parent or family member was sexual. If a parent is supposed to love you, and if parents are sexual with you, the conclusion is that this must be a part of the way a parent loves you. This is delusional thinking, but remember that it is a child doing it. These children may grow up to be sex addicts who think, "Sex is equal to love."

The experience of sex with a parent is frightening and painful. Sex addicts may come to believe that for sex to take place it must be mysterious, evil, uncomfortable, and dangerous. In fact, Dr. Patrick Carnes has said that for a sex addict, "For sex to be good, it has to be bad."

Cross Addictions

As a teenager, Barry drank alcohol with his friends and to loosen up before a date. When he got older he found that drinking allowed him to be more aggressive with women. This usually got him what he wanted— sex. Even though he got married, he continued to have affairs and his drinking progressed.

Barry's wife, who didn't know about the other women, demanded he stop drinking. Barry went to treatment for alcoholism and then regularly attended AA meetings. Although he stayed sober for years, he continued to have affairs, sometimes with other AA members. When he told his AA sponsor about his affairs, the man laughed and told Barry to do whatever it took to stop drinking.

Many sex addicts have cross addictions—they are addicted to other behaviors and substances. Sex is their primary addictive activity, but there are others. Many sex addicts who come for treatment, like Barry, are already recovering alcoholics. They may have experienced many years of sobriety from alcohol. They may even have thought that if they got sober from alcohol and drugs they would stop their sexual activities. Tragically, however, their sexual acting out got worse when they achieved alcoholic sobriety.

Some, while achieving sobriety from sex, struggle with compulsive eating. Many gain weight. Others continue to smoke heavily, spend compulsively, gamble, or watch TV incessantly. The list of possibilities is endless. I remember talking to one man who in one month had rented sixty videos, none of them R- or X-rated, from the local video store.

Sex addicts learn to escape their feelings through compulsive behavior or addictions. Many have several major addictions and a longer list of minor ones. Dr. Carnes has discovered in his research that the more severe the childhood abuse experience, the more likely it is that a sex addict will have multiple addictions.[2] This makes sense. The more painful the childhood experience, the more escapes an addict needs to medicate the pain.

In recovery, sex addicts may have trouble with other addictions, and there may be significant emotional and spiritual issues left to work on. If sex is the primary way addicts escape emotional and spiritual issues, stopping sex will only bring those issues to the surface. Addicts must first learn how to deal with emotional and spiritual issues in healthy ways before they can deal with the addiction itself.

Sex addicts may wonder, "When will all these addictions stop?" It is discouraging to battle many addictive behaviors, but they may suffer from what has been called an "addictive personality disorder."[3] People who are this addictive can abuse many behaviors or substances and easily become addicted to them if they are not careful.

Attention Disorders, Depression, and Anxiety

Sex addicts may suffer from a wide variety of classic mental health problems. Some of these may be manifestations of the same factors that led to addiction, and some may be the result of genetic problems in the neurochemistry of the brain.[4] This section reviews the three most common mental health conditions addicts suffer: attention disorders, depression, and anxiety.

In a recent study conducted with over 100 sex addicts, roughly 70 percent indicated Attention Deficit Disorder (ADD) might be an issue for them. ADD may actually represent a collection of disorders, all of them involving problems with attention, distraction, and organization. People who suffer with ADD may have a genetic or environmentally produced need for more regulation of the brain chemicals involved in the transmission and organization of thoughts. One of these chemicals, dopamine, is thought to be a primary factor in this problem. Various activities and substances, such as caffeine, nicotine, and adrenaline, can elevate dopamine. Danger and crisis stimulate adrenaline and thereby dopamine. Sexual activity and fantasy can also elevate dopamine.

What this suggests is that a brain that needs more dopamine is a brain that needs more stimulus. People who are addicted to smoking, caffeine, gambling (a dangerous or risky activity), and sex often tell me they are bored. Their brains need more stimulation. This begins to explain why many addicts have multiple addictions. They could be addicted to any substance or activity that elevates dopamine and provides the stimulation they crave. Appropriate medical treatment of attention problems can have an incredibly beneficial impact on sex addicts trying to control their sexual behaviors.

Anxiety and depression can be traced to difficult life situations, but can also be traced to chemical imbalances in the brain. The consequences of sexual sin may also create anxiety and depression, but chemical imbalances can cause a person to seek relief through sexual activity. Thus, while sexual sins can create anxiety and depression, they may also be considered the solution by addicts looking for relief. Such cyclical thinking leads to what is described as the sexual addiction cycle.

THE SEXUAL ADDICTION CYCLE

The behaviors and characteristics of sexual addiction can be understood by what Dr. Carnes has described as the Sexual Addiction Cycle. (See figure 2 on the next page.)

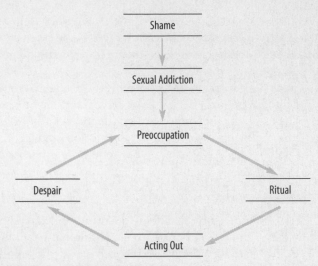

Figure 2: The Carnes Sexual Addiction Cycle

Sex addicts, like all addicts, are ashamed and seek to escape this feeling through addictive activity; however, that behavior in turn increases the sense of shame. Escaping shame through addiction that in turn increases shame is one cycle a sex addict experiences. This cycle needs to be understood to recover from sexual addiction.

The first part of the sexual addiction cycle is *preoccupation*. Rather than allowing themselves to experience their shame, pain, and loneliness, sex addicts start thinking about sex. Preoccupation involves the building-block behavior of sexual fantasy.

This preoccupation in itself produces pleasurable and exciting sensations, creating a positive mood in order to avoid a negative one. This behavior can be used at any time of the day in any situation. Often sex addicts may seem as though they are not mentally present as they are preoccupied with other thoughts.

Preoccupation also creates a desire to act out the thoughts. Before acting out can occur, a sex addict needs to plan. This phase of the sexual addiction cycle is called the *ritual*. Rituals are as varied in number as there are sex addicts. They may be very simple or very complex.

Addicts may come home at night, pick up the TV guide, look for provocative movies, and watch them. While at work, addicts may go into the bathroom to masturbate. They might also drive to the bank for money, and then cruise neighborhoods where they can purchase sex. When traveling, sex addicts might look for massage parlors in the phone book and call them to get prices. Many sex addicts have lists of available partners and have only to call, stop by, or otherwise make the connection with these partners to become sexual.

Rituals may take five minutes or five hours. Some sex addicts travel great distances to obtain pornography and won't act out with it until they return home. Some make elaborate travel plans to connect with partners from around the country or around the world. Sometimes the ritual involves accumulating nonsexual materials that are used in the sexual acting out. One sex addict always bought plastic sheets to cover his apartment so as not to "soil" it with his sexual activity.

Recruiting new partners creates rituals that may last for months and years. A man may meet a woman and at first simply engage her in conversation, telling her jokes that involve sexual humor. If she laughs, the conversation over time may regularly include this kind of teasing. He invites her to lunch, and the conversation begins to revolve around disclosing more intimate details of each other's lives.

At this point in the ritual, the two people consider themselves to be friends. They enjoy their sharing but begin to feel a certain excitement and sexual longing. Perhaps even years after their original conversation, they become sexual with each other. At the time when sex happens, the sex addict may think it happened all of a sudden and was "spontaneous." This is absurd. He or she has been soliciting this experience since the original meeting.

Just like the fantasies in the preoccupation stage, the ritual may in itself be exciting. This could be the excitement of the romance in discovering a new partner. It could be exciting to find some new form of pornography or a massage parlor that practices certain techniques the sex addict hasn't experienced before. Some sexual addiction cycles contain risk, like going to bars in dangerous neighborhoods or having secret meetings with potential partners. This danger and excitement produces adrenaline, which is itself addictive.

Once sex addicts have reached the ritual stage it is almost inevitable that they will go on to the next stage: *acting out*. I have previously described various kinds of acting out. Acting out does not just happen like a sudden thunderstorm. Conscious and unconscious thought is always behind it—preoccupation, preparation, and the ritual. When Christians say to a sex addict, "Stop acting out," they must also be prepared to help them stop thinking and planning.

Sexual addiction seems unmanageable because acting out seems to just "happen." Sex addicts must learn that this is not true. One addict recently described going to a distant city. When he got there, he got in his rental car, got cash from an ATM, and then drove to a massage parlor. "It was as if the car was on automatic pilot," he said. I asked him when he first knew he was going to this city. The answer was, months before. Had he ever been there before? Yes. Had he ever been to that massage parlor before? Yes. When did he start thinking about the possibility of going there again? Several weeks before the trip, he said. The reality is that he had been preoccupied with going to that massage parlor for weeks, made sure he had enough money in his account, and had his own car to get there! This acting out did not happen in a few minutes; it took several weeks.

Once acting out has occurred, the final stage of the cycle is *despair*. Sex addicts want to stop but, once again, they fail. They commit more shameful activity and now feel weak, perverted, and helpless. Anxious about being found out, they fall into a deep depression.

Despair is a form of depression. Many sex addicts are deeply depressed, although they may not be aware of it. Those around them certainly know that they have black moods, and might even question them about their moodiness. Sex addicts learn not to talk about their feelings so they deny this if asked. They also have great tolerance for pain and deny to themselves that they feel as badly as they do.

Depression at this level can lead to other problems, such insomnia, overeating or not eating, inability to concentrate, hypersensitivity, and mood swings. Most symptoms of depression express themselves physically in headaches, backaches, fatigue, and stomach disorders. Susceptibility to infections and even cancer can also result from chronic depression. I would wager to say that a majority of visits to a doctor's office are the result of depression-related physical symptoms.

Ultimately, the stage of despair leads to thoughts of suicide. The shame and hopelessness is so deep that the only way out seems to be death. If sexual addiction is in fact a disease, the ultimate consequence of any disease left untreated is death.

The despair may also be full of anger and blame. "It is God's fault, he didn't help me again." Or, "It was their fault, they seduced me again." Or, "It is my spouse's fault. If only she would be more sexual with me." Or, "If we could only get rid of the pimps, pornographers, and prostitutes, I would be all right." To a sex addict it may seem easier to control others, including culture itself, than to control oneself.

What are sex addicts to do about this despair? They do not know how to get help and are too ashamed to confess their activities to anyone who might help. To escape their despair then, they return to the old cycle of preoccupation with sex, ritual, acting out, and despair. The downward spiral begins anew.

OBSERVABLE SYMPTOMS

Although sex addicts attempt to conceal their behavior, they usually exhibit some readily observable symptoms. People who live, work, or worship with a sex addict might notice these. If you see someone exhibiting these symptoms, that person may need help and probably doesn't have the strength or tools to be able to ask for it.

As you read through these symptoms, be careful to avoid jumping to conclusions about the behavior of others. Some of these symptoms might indicate other addictions or emotional problems.

Here is a brief list of twelve observable symptoms of sexual addiction.

Preoccupation with Sexual Behaviors

Sex addicts are first of all extremely preoccupied with their own sexual fantasies. This preoccupation leads them to search for sexual expression of their fantasies. They devote more and more time to the preoccupation until they get to a point where sexual thoughts and activities are the central organizing principle of their lives.

There are many ways to observe this symptom. Is pornography of any type present? Does the person watch sexually explicit videos? Are X- or R-rated videos lying around? Does the person notice or point out sexually oriented places like bookstores, massage parlors, or striptease bars? Do they do double takes of attractive people? Does their conversation seem to center on sexual activity?

If you are this person's sexual partner, does he or she either ask for sex incessantly, or never ask? Does he or she complain about lack of sex or ask for sexual practices you don't enjoy?

These are some of the more obvious indications. In a more subtle way, if you live around a sex addict, you may sense a "feeling" of sexual energy. Even though you may not be aware of the sexual practices taking place, you have an intuitive sense that something is wrong.

Escalating Patterns of Sexual Activity

Sexual addiction is a degenerative disease, and the amount or level of activity increases over time. For example, it may seem normal to go to R-rated movies because lots of people do. In early stages, sex addicts may scan movie reviews to see which ones portray sex. From that they graduate to R-rated movies from the video store. Next, they move on to X-rated videos, and from there they may frequent more dangerous places for hard-core pornography.

The patterns of escalation can be as varied as the numbers of sex addicts. They may be short or long. They may vary in intensity. Remember that sex addicts can go for long periods of time without acting out. They may fool themselves or others into thinking their disease is under control. More serious behaviors may alternate with less serious ones. In fact, sex addicts may commit less serious behaviors to stop more serious ones, or reward themselves with lesser ones for not committing the more serious forms. This may allow them to delude themselves into thinking the pattern is not escalating. In the final analysis, however, the acting out always gets worse.

Acting Distant or Withdrawn

As the pattern of sexual activity escalates, sex addicts seem more distant and withdrawn because they are preoccupied with their sexual activity, guilt, shame, and fear of getting caught. They are unavailable mentally and often physically to everyone around them. They may seem distant or cold, or they may even become angry if badgered about what they are thinking. Ask them what the trouble is, and they deny any problem. More and more, their work, activity, interests, and relationships suffer from lack of attention.

Depression and Mood Swings

Sex addicts may be alternately depressed and then excited, even giddy. In the sexual addiction cycle, the withdrawn character of preoccupation is followed by the excitement of the ritual or the chase, the high of acting out, and then the despair or shame. Asking them about these mood changes elicits elaborate denials and perhaps even rage.

Irritability

Sex addicts try to avoid their feelings and avoid being found out. They create enormous defenses. If anyone asks questions that come too close to the truth or simply challenges their story, addicts can become greatly irritated. Their behavior makes them angry with themselves and angry with others. Past abuse issues also create hidden resentments and angers. Triggers that remind them of these past events may set off anger that seems unrelated to the importance of the event. Simple questions, insignificant events, or basic statements may incite an angry reaction that will surprise you because the reaction is out of proportion to the event.

Abuse of Self or Others

If sex addicts have been abused in the past, they may do the same to others. If they have not been talked to, they won't talk to others. If they have been yelled and screamed at, they yell and scream at others. If they have been preached to, they preach to others. They abuse others in ways they were abused. Victims of this abuse may believe this is acceptable behavior, or they may be too afraid or ashamed to confront it.

Sex addicts may also abuse themselves. Their personal habits and hygiene, their eating, smoking, and drinking, may annoy everyone around them. They may engage in any activity or use any substance compulsively. I met one sex addict who chewed three packs of gum while exercising for three hours every day.

Many sex addicts tell intimate details of their lives, except the sexual details, to strangers. A Catholic bishop told me about one priest who had almost every member of this church thinking he or she was the priest's personal confidant. When his sexual acting out was discovered, everyone was shocked by it and felt guilty they hadn't known. Sex addicts try to get people to like them by seeming to confide in them. Sex addicts have lots of acquaintances, but no friends.

Resistance to Supervision or Criticism

Since they hide a large part of their daily behaviors, sex addicts are not very open to criticism, whether or not it is constructively given. They may live with people who would very much like to correct their behaviors and who continue to turn up the volume of their criticisms in order to be heard. This just drives sex addicts deeper into withdrawal, for they do not want their sexual behaviors to be challenged.

Use of Sexual Humor

Sex addicts may use sexual humor all the time. They are always teasing (which many consider sexual harassment) or telling sexual jokes. Sex addicts sexualize most situations and see some sexual humor in it. Sexual jokes can be used to recruit new sexual partners. Sex addicts can gauge the reaction of a person hearing their sexual joke, and if that reaction is favorable, the level of sexual engagement might be taken one step higher.

Sex addicts are great at double entendre—words or phrases that might have two meanings, one of them sexual. Say something in this fashion and the sex addict will smile and point out the sexual content. If a person says, "My friend was able to get off on time this morning," a sex addict interprets "get off" to be about orgasm and makes some sexual joke about it.

Inappropriate Sexual Behavior and Overt Sexual Advances

Know what to look for and you can spot a sex addict at a party, the grocery store, even at church. They tell sexual jokes, they touch people in ways that don't feel right, they give too many hugs, and they are looking, always looking. Their eyes dart here and there. They take everything in. They follow certain attractive people.

Some sex addicts are very direct. They will come right up to you and talk about sex. One day the receptionist at a health club told me a man had just come up to her, out of the blue, and asked if she would like to go home with him. There are more subtle overtures than this, and sex addicts can be very creative.

As the disease progresses, inappropriate sexual behaviors get worse. A pastor's wife told me how her husband first took her to R-, then X-rated movies. Next he bought a video camera and wanted to film her nude. Then he wanted to film her being sexual with other men. When she refused, he became angry and abusive. She left, and he never has received help. The strange part about stories like this is how long it may take a loved one to challenge the behavior. Look for it in the early days. The progression of the disease means the consequences will get worse.

Spouses should be aware that sex addicts will become increasingly frustrated with sexual activity in marriage. They may avoid sex altogether because of frustration or as a result of sexual activity outside of marriage. Sex addicts may make increasing demands for sex and certain types of sexual activity, or they may not be interested in sex at all.

An uneducated spouse may feel guilty that he or she can't fulfill the marital "obligation," and feel angry at or repulsed by the demands. It is difficult for Christian spouses to confront inappropriate sexual demands in marriage because they may assume it is their duty to be submissive. However, they need to assert their right to have sexual standards and preferences.

An educated spouse knows that no amount of sexual activity or attractiveness is enough to satisfy an active sex addict. Even if the sex in marriage may seem quite good, he or she might not be aware of the partner's frustrations because the sex addict doesn't have the ability to articulate them.

Occupational, Social, Family, Professional, and Legal Difficulties

As the disease progresses, increasing amounts of time are spent thinking about and obtaining sex. This means less time for work, social life, family, professional responsibilities, or any other obligations. Ignoring these activities is evidence that energy is being drained off somewhere else. A concerned person should demand to know what is going on. Family members have a right to know because they are the victims.

If work is ignored, jobs and income will be lost. Friendships or other social relationships will be lost. Unethical conduct can result in the loss of professional licenses or the ability to practice the profession. If illegal behavior is involved, a sex addict may be arrested and could go to jail. Many sex addicts try to explain away arrests, such as soliciting prostitution, as isolated events that won't happen again. Don't be fooled! These arrests are rarely, if ever, isolated. More than likely they are part of a long-standing pattern.

Before the addict experiences great losses and consequences, look for signs that the addict is ignoring obligations, duties, jobs, and relationships. Even if you discern sexual addiction, you might not be able to help a sex addict. Some of them need to bottom out before they are willing to get help.

Intuition

This last symptom is observable not in the sex addict, but in those who are in relationship with the sex addict. Be an observer of your own intuition. Deb, my wife, calls it being a "gentle observer." This means taking your own feelings and perceptions seriously, and not being too hard on yourself for ignoring them in the past. Most spouses, bosses, pastors, or friends of sex addicts have a sixth sense that something is wrong. This may take various forms and could simply be a combination of impressions from certain events. Friends and family may feel they are not getting the full or the real story. The explanations of sex addicts for where they were or what they were doing on such-and-such an occasion just don't make sense.

One spouse told me her husband used to take thirty to forty-five minutes to take the baby-sitter home. He explained he was just visiting or that he had stopped off at the convenience store and then just driven around to relax. He sounded convincing and sincere, but it didn't make sense. In fact, he was briefly visiting a woman with whom he was having an affair.

Trust your instincts and act on them. Looking the other way and hoping things will get better is not a caring reaction, for the sex addict is slowly dying, and things will only get worse.

Direct Evidence

Perhaps the most obvious observable symptom, but often the one that shows up last, is direct evidence. Don't ignore the direct evidence: charge card bills from companies with strange names, phone bills with unfamiliar or 900 numbers, pornographic magazines, pornographic computer files, and so on. A spouse may be the last one to accept this evidence. A part of them doesn't want the pain of accepting the truth. The spouse may even become involved in elaborate explanations of why it can't be true. You may have heard the phrase, "the family is the last to know." Families often aren't the last to know, but they may be the last to accept the facts.

CONSEQUENCES

Stan was a pastor who had built up a strong and vital congregation. He had a loving wife and a daughter. They seemed to be a wonderful family. But Stan was addicted to pornography and prostitution. Over the years he squandered thousands of dollars to feed his sexual habits. To pay for his habits, he applied for and received a number of charge cards. Finally, he could no longer pay his bills. His balance on all of these cards was $40,000.

Stan was desperate. How could he tell his wife or his church about these bills? He once worked for a bank and knew how they operated. He bought a cheap handgun, began robbing banks, and paid his debts.

After he robbed his twelfth bank he was caught. This fine pastor went to federal prison for eight years because of his addiction to pornography and prostitution.

Sex addicts routinely run the risk of all kinds of consequences. For some, the danger of their activities is part of the high. They risk AIDS and other infectious diseases. They risk the loss of jobs, career, spouse, friends, and money. They may be arrested, sued, or jailed. Depression, anxiety, and other emotional conditions also result. Often sex addicts get so involved in flurries of activity they become exhausted and burned out. Fatigue and exhaustion in turn lead to a host of physical illnesses and symptoms.

Physical injury is also common. The pastor's wife mentioned earlier masturbated so regularly she needed surgical repair. Suicide is the ultimate consequence. Consider the case of Paul, a youth pastor. He was addicted to pornography since the age of eleven. As an adult, he became involved with pornography featuring teenage girls. His deep involvement in this form of pornography led him to become sexually involved with a sixteen-year-old girl in his youth group. He was eventually reported and arrested. Before he went to trial for his crime, he committed suicide rather than face the consequences.

Consequences do not stop the addict from acting out. I have known several sex addicts who have been sexual with persons they knew had AIDS. This is how desperate addicts become to obtain their "supply," and it is another example of suicidal thinking.

If you suspect someone you know is a sex addict, there are things you can do to help. We'll discuss them in part three: "Healing the Wounds of Sexual Addiction." But first, it's important to understand the roots of sexual addiction—where it comes from and what causes it, which is the subject of the next chapter.

PART II

THE ROOTS OF SEXUAL ADDICTION

CHAPTER 5

UNHEALTHY
FAMILY DYNAMICS

Sexual addiction begins in families that possess unhealthy dynamics and characteristics.

Take the case of Roger. On the surface, Roger's family seemed a model one. Roger's dad was a busy, successful businessman who was involved in numerous civic activities. The whole family was very active in their local church.

Roger, the oldest son, was a star athlete and good student. After high school, Roger was expected to enter his father's business. When he graduated, he started doing various jobs around one of his father's factories. Eventually, Roger married a woman with two daughters.

Underneath, however, Roger's family was far from perfect. Very unhealthy dynamics were going on. Roger's mother fondled his genitals when he was between the ages of one and three. Later, one of his uncles made him perform oral sex. An aunt had intercourse with Roger when he was a teenager. Roger had an ongoing sexual relationship with a sister one year younger than himself until they both left home. In the factory, Roger's father, normally passive at home, yelled and screamed at him when he didn't get something quite right. One of the ways Roger coped was by drinking alcohol. As he grew older this problem got worse.

The drinking problem was more easily recognizable so Roger began going to Alcoholics Anonymous. He achieved sobriety, yet still masturbated daily, shopped X-rated bookstores, frequented prostitutes, and had a string of affairs. His wife found out about one of the affairs and demanded that he change. His pastor encouraged him to be gentle with himself, to accept God's forgiveness, and to work on his marriage so as to remain faithful.

In Roger's "perfect family," neither sex nor problems of any kind were ever talked about. Everyone was expected to perform in ways that were acceptable and admirable to the outside community. While Roger's family seemed wonderful to everyone else, the family members were distant and cold. Roger remembers masturbating alone in his room at the age of five. His mother had demonstrated to him at an early age how pleasurable this sensation felt, and he soon learned to use it to escape the loneliness and chaos of his family.

UNDERSTANDING WOUNDS THAT FAMILIES CREATE

Roger's story is not unique. Like most sex addicts, Roger grew up in a family that had many unhealthy dynamics. While his family appeared normal to the outside world, family members were strangers, even enemies, to each other. Roger cannot recover from his sexual addiction until he understands the nature of the pain he felt growing up in this family.

Saying that a family has unhealthy qualities, like Roger's, is not being judgmental. It is being descriptive. Members of Roger's family committed many immoral behaviors that should be judged as such. We can judge behaviors and seek to understand them, but we shouldn't judge people. Many parents are doing the best they can. Many families make unhealthy mistakes out of loving intentions. However, if parents have not learned how to give love in healthy ways, and if family members have not attained some degree of personal health and maturity, it is highly likely that the whole family system will be affected.

Labeling a family as either "healthy" or "unhealthy" isn't necessarily helpful. Many Christians get stuck in black-and-white thinking trying to decide if their families are "good" or "bad." Ultimately, these distinctions are meaningless. All families have good and bad, healthy and unhealthy, qualities. All families and all family members make mistakes. These mistakes create wounds in a human spirit. These wounds may be emotional, physical, sexual, or spiritual.

Sex addicts attempt to escape family wounds and associated painful feelings by creating pleasurable feelings through sexual activity. It is important for sex addicts to recognize that their sexual activity is an attempt to medicate old wounds and to find love. To begin, they must identify and understand their wounds. Understanding wounds leads sex addicts back to their childhood family dynamics. Understanding these dynamics begins the process of healing.

Sex addicts in recovery from their disease do not blame family members for their addiction. Nor do they seek to avoid their own responsibility for getting well. Recovering addicts, however, must acknowledge the wounds they suffered and understand that they didn't deserve them. They must admit they did not receive the love and nurture they needed, and that many of the messages they learned may have been wrong. Understanding these things is crucial to changing opinions of themselves and others. It is also crucial in finding the love and nurturing they never got but always needed.

Wounds "filter" the truth about who a person really is. In Psalm 139, we read that we are "fearfully and wonderfully made," and that God knows us from the moment of conception. From John 3:16 we know that God so loved us that he sent his only Son to die for us. Addicts must ask themselves if their families helped or hindered them from understanding these basic truths. God really loves us. We are all really special to him. If the people around us aren't good at modeling that love, it may impair us from truly understanding God. It is like a coffee filter. You put coffee grounds in the filter and when you pour water through it you get coffee. Our human spirits and our minds have filters. When you put various forms of abuse into them, you can pour the living water (John 4) of Christ's love into them but what comes out is still tainted with core beliefs that we are bad and worthless people.

When addicts identify their wounds, they may become angry and need to grieve. It may take a number of years to work through this process because it stirs up powerful emotions.

Jesus told Nicodemus that to inherit the kingdom of God we must be born again (John 3:3). We must become like a child seeking God's nurturing care. For abuse victims, this thought can be extremely painful.

However, becoming a child again can be healing if we understand and embrace the pain and begin to work through it. Jesus beckons the little children to come to him (Matthew 19:14), and he calls us his brothers and sisters. While our earthly family is imperfect, our heavenly Father is perfect. Knowing God the Father can allow us the freedom to accept our memories, to be born again, and to take comfort in him.

If you are an addict, this chapter and the next one may stir up painful memories. Don't run from them. Talk to someone who will listen and accept you. If necessary, get counseling from someone who knows how to work through these feelings.

In his ministry on earth, Jesus cast out demons that had possessed their victims and controlled their lives. Painful childhood memories are often like those demons. They are buried inside, and often people don't remember they are there. These unconscious memories of past events cause people to react in certain ways to current situations. The next two chapters name some of these demons from the past in order to help the sex addict get well. When sex addicts know their demons, they can make healthy choices about getting rid of them.

FOUR CATEGORIES THAT CONTRIBUTE TO UNHEALTHY FAMILY DYNAMICS

What constitutes unhealthy family dynamics? There are four categories of family dynamics that are helpful in answering this question: boundaries, rules, roles, and addictions (see figure 3). In this chapter we begin to understand the factors in a sex addict's family that make it vulnerable to experiences of abuse and wounds. This chapter and the next describe qualities of any unhealthy family, whether or not addiction is involved. For sex addicts, these dynamics are what lead to a sense of shame, loneliness, isolation, anger, and anxiety.

Boundaries

All families have boundaries. Boundaries are invisible areas of emotional, physical, sexual, and spiritual territory that exist around a person's

Boundaries	Rules	Roles	Addictions	
Loose	Don't talk	Hero	Substance	Behavioral
Rigid	Don't feel	Scapegoat	Alcohol	Sex
	Blame others	Mascot	Drugs	Work
	Minimize	Lost child	illegal	Gambling
	Deny	Doer	prescription	Spending
		Enabler	over the counter	Shopping
		Little prince/princess	Nicotine	Eating
		Saint	Caffeine	Stealing
			Food	Cleaning

Figure 3: Unhealthy Family Dynamics

body, mind, and soul. They are like a force field. They are your "space." Boundaries define the ways a person's invisible space can and can't be crossed. When boundaries are maintained in a healthy way, a person feels safe and protected. A family that touches each other in healthy ways and doesn't touch each other in sexual ways gives family members a sense of being safe and loved. This is a nurturing environment.

Boundaries are described as "loose" when interactions that shouldn't happen take place between family members. Boundaries are violated. One evening a friend of mine accidentally walked into his teenaged daughter's room while she was getting undressed. Although he left immediately, they were both embarrassed because he crossed an invisible boundary line. The unspoken boundary is that teenagers need privacy, and he should have knocked before entering her room.

Boundary violations are more serious in families in crisis. Members of these families are hit, yelled at, sexually touched, or preached at inappropriately. When boundaries are too loose, people learn that they don't have control over their bodies, minds, or spirits. Others invade their privacy. Someone older, someone bigger, someone they trust, does things to them, and they can't stop it. Even saying no does no good. They find the only way to please the other person is to cooperate, to open their boundaries, and to let the other person abuse them. These experiences affect how people relate to others, especially to loved ones and family, for the rest of their lives.

Boundaries can also become too rigid. Healthy interactions that should occur, don't. Loving and caring, listening and nurturing, guiding and witnessing, teaching and modeling, do not take place. Children in these families feel as if they are held at arm's length. Starved for affection and attention, they begin to wonder, "What's wrong with me? I must be a bad person. Mom and Dad don't love me." To whom can these lonely children talk? They have learned that no one will listen. They feel abandoned. Later in life, they will seek to fill their loneliness with inappropriate and sinful behaviors.

Both loose and rigid boundaries can exist in the same family. One parent may cross a loose boundary while another observes a rigid boundary. The child experiences both simultaneously. At different times, different family members can be involved in this mixture of loose and rigid boundaries. The same person who commits incest can at other times be totally loving. He or she violates boundaries that should be in place and creates other boundaries that should exist.

When families demonstrate both loose and rigid boundaries, children are confused. The models they see are inconsistent and unpredictable. Later in life, when these children (now adults) break some rule, someone may ask, "Didn't you know any better?" They may have known better intellectually, but were confused emotionally. Dave, for example, was molested by his mother when he was a child. His mother was otherwise a very loving and caring person. Dave was confused about the relationship between a mother's love and sex. After a long history with pornography and masturbation, Dave perpetrated incest on his daughter. Intellectually, he knew it was wrong, but the emotional confusion about what a parent does led him into this abusive sin. Dave's situation is what some refer to as the "victim to victimizer cycle." It is also what the Bible refers to as the sins of the father being passed down for generations.

A prosecuting attorney asked a pastor, "Do you know which commandment says not to commit adultery?" The pastor did. The attorney then asked, "If you knew, why did you violate it?" The pastor knew right from wrong in his mind, but he had grown up with incest and other forms of sexual sin. In his experience, so many sexual boundaries had been crossed that he was emotionally confused about right and wrong.

Boundary confusion can be taught in more subtle ways than incest. I took my eight-year-old son to an air show where the ticket price for children seven and under was only two dollars. I was tempted to tell the ticket taker that he was seven, but if I had done so, I would have been teaching my son that in our family we can break rules. In major or minor ways, when otherwise loving parents either model breaking boundaries or don't protect us in ways they should, we can wind up confused about healthy love and nurture.

Families that practice healthy relationships work to guard and nurture boundaries. Growing up in this kind of family creates a feeling of being safe and loved.

Rules

It is healthy to learn how to accept and talk about pain and feelings of loneliness, fear, anxiety, and anger. Contrary to unhealthy beliefs, talking about feelings does not make them worse. Family members might say, "If I talk about my anger, it will get out of control—I might kill someone." The healing journey away from sexual addiction involves lots of talking and lots of feelings. It involves taking responsibility for one's actions. Addicts who want to heal need to learn new rules of behavior and family dynamics.

Some families have rules of conduct to prevent tension from getting out of control. These rules are probably never spoken or written down, but the whole family knows them and acts accordingly. Here are five of the most common:

We Don't Talk

Families may talk about superficial matters like the weather, sports, or a TV show, but they certainly don't talk about feelings, problems, or embarrassing situations. Adults readily offer pat solutions to prohibit other family members from expressing emotions. If members try to talk about something meaningful, they are ignored, teased, belittled, or simply told to be quiet. They might be told, "Big boys don't cry," or "Your brother never had a problem with that." Sometimes they offer compensation to avoid talking about emotions: "I know your dog died. I'll get you a new one. It will be all right." Religion may be brought into it: "God doesn't like it when you are so sad." The rule may be proudly and simply verbalized, "In this family we don't talk about that," whatever "that" may be.

We Don't Feel

This rule is specific to emotions. The feelings of family members are discouraged, particularly "negative" ones like anger, sadness, fear, or anxiety. The intent behind this rule is to be caring, but it becomes a form of denial. When a negative feeling surfaces, the guardian of the we-don't-feel rule might say, "Please don't feel that way. Let me help you solve your problems." This is unhealthy because when people are talked out of their feelings, the feelings don't go away. They stay buried inside the person as long as they remain unexpressed. Buried feelings may be unconscious, but they can affect behavior for many years.

We Blame Others for Our Problems

Unhealthy family members do not accept responsibility for their own problems or mistakes. To do so would create guilt over making a mistake and fear that someone will be mad at them or that something bad will happen. These families search for a scapegoat. A member might say, "You make me feel so angry." A healthy family member might say, "When you did that, I got angry. My anger belongs to me. I'd like to talk about what it was all about." Said in this way, the other person doesn't have to be defensive.

Direct statements of blame are heard every day in the school yard: "He hit me first. I had to hit him back," or "He called me a name. I had to push him." Individuals, groups, and institutions are often the object of this blame. I remember getting off the hook for poor performance in the fourth grade by blaming my teacher for being inept, old, senile, and a Catholic who had it in for preachers' kids like me!

We Minimize Our Problems

"That wasn't so bad," or "That was no big deal," is what we say when we are trying to convince others and ourselves that we aren't hurting or that we haven't hurt someone else. This is based on the perceived value of being of good courage, of not being a complainer, or of being a mature person. It can also be based on the belief that we are good people and we don't cause harm to others. We create elaborate explanations for why things are really better than they seem. For example, "Think of all those people in India who don't have any food to eat or clothes to wear. We should be thankful for what we do have."

Healthy family members don't minimize problems, they accept them. They place them in proper perspective and search for appropriate solutions while at the same time accepting the painful feelings the problems may create. A healthy family member might say, "That must really hurt. I'd like to hear about that. I'd also like to talk with you about ways we might try to prevent it from happening in the future."

We Deny Our Problems

Some family members deny they have difficulties or have caused harm to themselves or to someone else. Family members might simply say, "I didn't mean to," or "I'm sorry. You'll forgive me won't you?" or "Why are you so upset? That was no big deal." What these statements really mean is, "Don't blame me. It's not my fault. Don't be angry with me. Get off my back!" We think that if we deny our problems, we won't have to feel the pain of them.

Denial often takes the form of elaborate deceptions: lying, covering up, or looking the other way. For example, "That wasn't my car you saw at the motel," or "I was at the office working late on the books; it's almost tax time you know," or "I really don't know what you're talking about. I wasn't there."

The health of a family is a relative matter. There may be times when not talking about something is appropriate—to avoid unnecessary hurt or embarrassment, or to maintain legitimately confidential information. Sometimes trying not to feel so bad or temporarily minimizing a problem are positive strategies that enable us to get through a difficult time. Feelings can be talked about later when there is more time or when it is safer to do so. There are times when someone really has done something wrong and deserves to be blamed or at least held accountable for the actions. This can be done in love and not in judgment. But there are also times when a person has done nothing wrong and needs to deny it to an angry accuser.

Roles

Roles are like parts in a play, defining the "job description" of each family member. Roles provide clear expectations of how to act in all family situations. They are given to a family member in spoken and unspoken ways. Roles are unhealthy when they are inflexible and when they prevent someone from becoming the person God intends for them to be. Sex addicts may experience sadness, anger, and resentment about the roles they play. This is fuel for addiction. Roles also influence the choices we make about the people we choose to be around in life, where we work, and even where we might go to church.

Roles are assigned at birth. The first child may be assigned to fulfill certain long-awaited expectations. Names may even illustrate what the family might hope for the child: "My grandfather John was a great man and a great lawyer; let's name our first son John." Maybe this new John doesn't want to be a great man or a great lawyer, but this is the role he is assigned.

The stories families tell about each other, the world, their values and opinions are small and continual reminders of role expectations. Our new John may hear about his great-grandfather's wonderful exploits, noble character, and powerful legal adventures. The family extols the virtues of a law career. On family vacations, John's parents point out every law school they pass. Later in life, when John wonders about all of this, his parents might say, "We never told you to be a lawyer." Maybe they didn't directly, but their indirect communication clearly set up the explanation that he would become one.

Roles are also based on what the family needs the child to be to maintain family functions. Some roles are culturally defined, such as the gender expectations routinely placed on boys and girls. Families, schools, the media, movies, TV, and church present models of how men and women behave. We are all influenced by the culture we grew up in. If you are a parent, do you not wonder how our culture is influencing your children?

Sometimes modeling is based on deeply held beliefs. There are churches that don't allow women to serve in leadership positions based on their interpretation of certain Scripture passages. When my wife and I lived for a time in Iowa, there were still schools that had half-court basketball rules for girls. It was believed that girls didn't have the stamina to run back and forth on a full court so these schools had six-person teams—three girls played offense and three girls played defense. No one was allowed to cross the half-court line.

Many authors have written about a variety of roles in family systems. I have distilled these into eight primary roles.[1] As you read this section you might want to write down what your family looks like. Diagram your family on a piece of paper like you would draw a family tree. Write in everyone's name and leave enough room under each to make notes. As you read the role descriptions below, consider if the characteristics of each role apply to any members of your family. Remember that we all play several roles and each role can be played by more than one person.

The Hero

Family heroes are expected to always excel. They are scholars, athletes, or social stars. They are always right, and the family turns to them for answers. As heroes play their roles, they assume authority and achieve special status. More time, attention, and money is devoted to their lessons, education, and activities. The rest of the family may be secretly jealous but never talks about these feelings. Instead, everyone in the family points to the hero and says, "See, we have this special person. We are a special family."

Families create elaborate stories around heroes. At holiday times and other family gatherings, members recount the hero's achievements, victories, accomplishments, and successes. They pass around pictures, display medals, hang diplomas with care, and neatly clip and save newspaper clippings.

The Scapegoat

Scapegoats are the opposite of heroes. Scapegoats are expected to make mistakes, to be wrong, and to be perpetually in trouble. Their mistakes don't have to be major—just big enough to attract attention to their stupidity or ineptness. Scapegoats are not expected to have talents or abilities, and they learn to hide gifts they do possess.

A family may feel it needs a scapegoat on whom to blame their problems. Somehow, consciously or unconsciously, the scapegoat learns this. What may later seem to be intentional or accidental mistakes could, in fact, be the result of learned patterns of reaction. Ultimately, the family may ostracize the scapegoat or he or she may even choose to leave, thus earning the label "black sheep" of the family.

The Mascot

Mascots are the family comedians. Mascots may tell a joke, say something sarcastic, make fun of themselves or someone else, or get into mischief to get people to laugh. This behavior deflects attention away from feelings and does, in fact, relieve tension. For example, any sexual feelings or tension in the family will be dispelled with a sexual joke.

Humor in itself is not bad. Healthy families frequently laugh with each other. At appropriate times humor relieves tension and can bring healing. Because an unhealthy family does not like to express feelings, mascots use humor to avoid them. They get people to smile or laugh, but they bury their feelings. The feelings don't go away but wait beneath the surface to explode perhaps days, weeks, months, and even years later.

The Lost Child

The lost child learns that the family doesn't express feelings, and his or her feelings are especially not to be heard. As a result, lost children learn to bury their feelings. They go to their rooms and read books or play quietly. They may have imaginary friends and talk to them in a language only they understand. To the outside world and to the family, they may be quiet or serious children, but they are more than this. Lost children are lost to themselves and to others, possessing deep feelings they learn how to numb because no one will listen. Because there is no one to talk to, they gradually don't even recognize that they have feelings.

Later in life they may seem like strong silent types. They may even be admired for their ability to maintain their composure. They are often considered to be strong people who can handle anything. If people ask them how they are, they quickly respond that they're fine. Lost children are set up to develop addictions of all kinds. They discover that an addictive substance or activity helps them to numb their feelings. Lost children are lonely, sad, and sometimes depressed.

The Doer

The doer is the family member who gets things done. Doers keep the family functioning by cooking the meals, paying the bills, doing the laundry, cleaning the house, and chauffeuring the kids. They love being busy.

If doers feel they are doing all the work, they may express this feeling in brief outbursts of anger or moodiness, but they go right on doing what they do. Sometimes doers even play a complaining game: "Nobody ever helps around here. I always wash the clothes." When someone offers to help, doers turn down the offer and do it themselves. Doers know that only they can do it right. In the complaining game doers may develop another identity, that of a martyr. In the martyr role, the doing remains constant with the added element of perpetual complaining. The doer is also set up to later become a workaholic.

The Enabler

This role is often used to describe the person who lives with an alcoholic and does nothing to confront the drinking. The same holds true in sexual addiction. The enabler tolerates inappropriate sexual behavior and does nothing to confront it. Enablers feel they wouldn't have an identity if they weren't somehow related to the addict.

Lies and excuses are the enabler's tools. They like to give the impression their family is "normal." Outsiders may wonder why the enabler puts up with things as they are. The solutions seem so obvious to anyone not so invested or enmeshed in the family: Get out! Enablers may have to deal with well-meaning friends who openly offer this solution.

In the Christian community, enablers may seem like saints. We might ask, "How do they put up with that craziness? It takes real faith, courage, and love to live like that!"

The Little Princess/Prince

On the surface, this role may seem similar to the hero. The main difference is that while the hero is expected to achieve and accomplish, the little princess/prince is expected to look good. The little princess or prince is expected to be warm and wonderful, cute and cuddly, and to exemplify to the world that only a special family could produce such a dream child. This child learns to smile, to dress in the best clothes, and to perform little songs and dances at the request of parents. The job of the little prince or princess is to entertain and please others.

Whatever feelings may be going on inside, the little princess or prince learns to hide them to always seem happy. These children grow up to be the kind of people everyone likes. They are charming, poised, polite, and graceful. They have charisma. An intuitive observer may sense a false front, but being the little princess or prince, like all the other roles, is learned early and played well at great sacrifice to emotional well-being.

The Saint

The saint is the family hero who is expected to be perfect in a religious way. The family may have some religious persuasion or none at all, yet the saint is exemplary of things deep, philosophical, and spiritual. All religious tasks of the family—praying, going to church, reading the Bible, or participating in other religious activities—are initiated by or performed by the saint.

Saints may be expected to enter a religious occupation. Many pastors, priests, nuns, and rabbis followed their families' expectations in choosing to enter the ministry. They may not have done this consciously, but somewhere inside they felt the directing to be ordained. This may not be the calling of God but the calling of the family. The saint may have other abilities and talents and never get to use them.

Combining Roles

In most families, more than one person can play the same role. Persons can also switch back and forth between roles. And the same person can play more than one role. In fact, most families are comprised of people playing combinations of roles. The doer and the enabler are frequently combined. Doing all the family functions enables others not to do them. The mascot can be combined with any of the other roles. The hero can be great at cracking jokes. The saint can be played in tandem with the hero or the little princess/prince. One of the ways a saint can learn his or her role is by performing little prince or princess activities at church. Any combination is possible.

Many pastors play the hero–saint–lost child. They are put on a pedestal (the hero); they are expected to be perfectly religious (the saint); and they spend lots of time alone (the lost child). This combination of roles is tragically lonely. When pastors have committed sexual sins, the hero–saint–lost child role combination prevents them from getting help.

All of us continue to play our roles after we leave our families. At work, we find we interact with our bosses and coworkers similarly to the ways we interacted with family members. In church, we play roles learned from childhood. While the pastor plays the hero-saint, many of us play the doers. In marriage we look for partners to play roles that complement ours. A hero, for example, will marry a doer-enabler, someone who keeps things running smoothly while the hero is out collecting accolades.

Addictions

Some families are full of addicts of one kind or another. Sex addicts come from families in which there is at least one other addict present. Since one of the main functions of unhealthy families is to keep feelings buried, many family members must work together to keep them buried. Family members can turn to addictions to accomplish this ongoing burial, since the main function of addiction is to escape or numb feelings.

There are two kinds of addictions: substance and behavioral. Substance addiction involves ingesting or taking a substance such as drugs or alcohol into the body. Behavior addiction involves repetitively performing behaviors such as sexual activity. See figure 3 for a partial list of these addictions.

Any substance or activity might be addictive. The key is whether or not something has become repetitive in an unmanageable way, is used for the purpose of escaping feelings, and has led or will lead to destructive consequences. Many of the chemicals or behaviors that can be addictive might not be evil in themselves. Sex is a God-given, natural, and beautiful activity. Addictions take place when even normal substances and activities become repeated in unmanageable and destructive ways.

Addictions in families are frequently used as stress management strategies. When a family member expresses boredom, loneliness, sadness, anger, or fear (all stressful emotions), another family member might respond, "Can I fix you something to eat?" or "Why don't you watch TV," or "Take a good stiff drink; that will cure what ails you." These are invitations to manage stressful feelings with behaviors and substances. These stress management strategies alter moods or at least take people's minds off their feelings. These forms of stress management can become addictive, particularly if used repeatedly by an impressionable child.

The addicts in a family may not think they are out of control with their behaviors. It is likely, however, that family members feel uncomfortable with them. However, the unspoken family rule overrides any discomfort and translates into, "We don't confront these behaviors because we want to keep things running smoothly. We don't want the outside world to know about our problems."

Family members might also deny their addiction and create elaborate delusions to explain away addictive activity. Some family members may initiate their own addictive behaviors as a way to cope with feelings they can't express or don't recognize, such as the pain of seeing one of the family slowly killing him- or herself. The spouse of a sex addict, for example, may become an overeater or a workaholic. In many families there are multiple addictions practiced simultaneously as family members slowly die of pain, loneliness, and addiction.

It is in the deep and fertile ground of chaos, dysfunction, silence, and abuse that the seeds of sexual addiction are sown. Sex addicts must begin their recovery by understanding what their families were like. How were the boundaries violated? How were the rules communicated verbally and nonverbally? What roles did they play? What addictions were present and how were they modeled?

These are painful questions to ask. In fact, as you think about this, a voice inside your head may be saying, "Those things aren't true about my family. It wasn't so bad. Don't be critical of my family; after all, they really loved me." I invite you to put these internal voices on hold as you continue to read in search of solutions to sexual addiction. It is especially hard for Christians to think critically about our families. We are taught to honor our fathers and mothers. There is a part of us that doesn't want things to have been so bad. The main thing to remember is that these issues are not black and white. Loving and good parents make mistakes. Most parents love their children and do the best they can. One benefit of trying to understand these issues is that understanding enables us to decide what kind of person, parent, spouse, or friend we want to be now and in the future.

HEALTHY FAMILY DYNAMICS

Boundaries	**Rules**	**Roles**	**Healthy Choices**
• Flexible	• We talk	• Interchangeable	• Instead of addictions, family members deal with stress, anxiety, fear, sadness, and anger by making healthy choices to self-nurture and ask for help
• Care and nurture are provided	• We feel	• The Hero, Saint, Mascot and Doer are played by each member at appropriate times	
• Respect for personal boundaries	• We accept our problems	• Enabling means caring, encouraging, and affirming	
	• We honestly evaluate the nature of our problems	• No Scapegoats, Little Prince/Princess, or Lost Children	
	• We take responsibility for our own actions		
	• We ask for help		

HEALTHY NURTURE

Emotional	**Physical**	**Sexual**	**Spiritual**
• Affirmations are given	• Safety is felt	• People's bodies are respected	• Personal spirituality is modeled
• Feelings are accepted	• Basic needs are provided	• Intimacy is modeled and taught	• Spiritual discipline is taught
• People are listened to	• Physical self-care is modeled and taught	• Sex education is provided	• Relationship to God based on love, not fear, is encouraged
• Individuality is encouraged			• Biblical and theological information and teaching is provided

HEALTHY SHAME

HEALTHY SELF

Empowerment
- Recognizes need for God and others
- Affirms self while understanding the unmanageability of one's life
- Discovers God's will for oneself

Self-care
- Makes healthy choices
- Nurtures self
- Has intimate relationships
- Asks for help

LOVE, JOY, PEACE

Figure 4: Healthy Families

HEALTHY FAMILIES

Healthy families do exist. Even people who come from relatively unhealthy families may strive to create their own healthy family. Many recovering sex addicts are succeeding at this.

The easiest way to understand a healthy family is to reverse the unhealthy characteristics. Figure 4 takes the family model and substitutes healthy dynamics for unhealthy ones.

In healthy families the cornerstone is healthy boundaries. These are flexible. As Ecclesiastes 3 says, there is a time for everything under God's heaven. In healthy families there is a time to touch and a time not to touch. This depends on the intention of the touch. If it is selfishly or sexually motivated, the boundary needs to be high. If it is respectful and nurturing, the boundary can be crossed. In a healthy family a person has a right to his or her own emotional, physical, sexual, and spiritual privacy. If a person in the family wants to cross this privacy boundary, it can be done for nurturing intentions. However, it is still necessary to ask permission, even if a privacy boundary is crossed for good intentions.

My daughter, now an adult, recently called me to ask my opinion about an issue. In order to give her more intelligent feedback I had to ask for some information that would otherwise be private. I did not assume I had the right to ask for this information, so I first asked for permission to even ask the question. Believe me, this is a lesson I have learned the hard way.

The rules in healthy families become positive prescriptions, not negative prohibitions. We talk and feel, we accept and honestly evaluate our problems, we take responsibility for our own behaviors, and we ask for help when we need it.

Roles are interchangeable. No one person plays them all the time. For example, all members can at times be the hero or the doer. Members share responsibility for getting things done. Achievements and recognitions are passed around. Humor is used in non-shaming ways to have fun and enjoy life. Everyone gets a turn at being the mascot. We are all saints. People share the responsibility for modeling healthy spirituality. Enabling becomes a positive virtue of caring, encouraging, and affirming. There are no scapegoats because everyone takes responsibility for his or her own behaviors and doesn't blame others. No one gets lost.

Everyone's needs are attended to. Members don't isolate themselves, but seek help when they need it.

Instead of using addictions to cope with stress and emotions, members of healthy families are taught how to make healthy choices about expressing feelings, solving problems, and nurturing themselves. Experiencing the full range of emotions is not discouraged. If there have been addicted members of the family, they are in recovery. They model sober behaviors and do the things to take care of themselves that will help keep them healthy.

Emotionally, members are affirmed for who they are and for their talents. They are encouraged to talk about and work through feelings, and these feelings are respected. A parent might say to a child, "You seem angry. Can you talk about that anger?" A person who has opportunities to express anger verbally doesn't need to raise the volume or do something physical in order to be heard or noticed.

Family members feel safe physically, and parents teach and model positive physical self-care. Sexually healthy families respect each other's bodies as being the temple of the Holy Spirit. Intimacy is present between parents. Sexual information is openly and appropriately discussed.

Healthy families worship a loving God. They read and teach Scripture. They practice spiritual disciplines and celebrate the joy of God's creation. Parents don't just send the kids off to church but are also involved themselves.

Such families are full of joy and gladness. They help to create people who have a healthy sense of self. Healthy shame is present, but this means that people honestly know their God-given talents, their human limitations, and their need for God and for other people. They understand that their lives are unmanageable without God.

Such a healthy self results in personal empowerment. Healthy family members have an ability to like themselves and to discover God's will for their lives. Healthy selves are also able to nurture themselves, to do nice things for themselves, to understand what they like, to pursue their interests, and to ask for help when they need it. They are capable of intimate relationships. In short, they are able to "love others as they love themselves."

Such families are wonderful to be a part of. Healthy families prevent the cycle of abuse from being passed down from generation to generation.

FAMILY ABUSE

Joe and his wife, Mary, have been fighting about sex for years. Ever since the honeymoon, Joe has demanded it, and Mary usually refuses. Then Joe feels rejected, hurt, and very angry, while Mary feels demeaned, manipulated, and also very angry. Their arguments have become volatile and destructive, and both feel guilty that they can't please each other. They think they have a terrible marriage because their sex life is so empty. Joe is also a sex addict. He masturbates, uses pornography, and goes to prostitutes.

The intensity of this argument is based on old wounds incurred in their families. Joe was emotionally abandoned by his mother, who never had much time for him. Mary was repeatedly raped by her father between the ages of twelve to sixteen. When Joe demands sex, Mary remembers of the trauma of incest. And when she says no, it reminds Joe of being pushed away from his mother. Joe does not go to a prostitute because he needs sex and can't have it with Mary. Rather, he is searching for the love and nurturing he didn't get from his family.

UNDERSTANDING FAMILY ABUSE

Joe and Mary illustrate why it is so important to understand unhealthy family dynamics. Family abuse is the damage or wounds done to a member of a family by another member of the family. These wounds negatively affect this member for the rest of his or her life unless he or she understands them and heals from them. Healing for sexual addiction can only begin when a person comes to a conscious awareness of what happened to them in childhood.

The cycle of abuse is vicious. Most people who abuse have been abused themselves. In many families the trail of abuse extends back for generations. Abuse is one vehicle whereby the "sins of the father" (or the mother) are passed down from one generation to the next.

The Old Testament clearly shows that the sins of the parents bring misfortune to future generations (Exodus 20:5), and the sins of the father and mother should not be forgotten (Psalm 109:14). David's sexual sin with Bathsheba left a legacy of sexual problems, including incest and murder.

Christians may wonder if sex addicts aren't just trying to blame their families or their abusers for their behaviors. The fact is that unrecovered sex addicts do indeed blame lots of other people, including parents. However, blame for the purpose of blame is unhealthy and, in fact, violates the commandment to honor mothers and fathers.

We describe abuse for the purpose of understanding, not for the purpose of blaming. Understanding implies healing. Blame implies judgment. Recovering sex addicts seek to understand their abuse in order to heal from it. But they should not use this understanding to blame others for their own behaviors.

To understand the abuse and heal from it, the victim will need to be angry. The victim will also need to confront the parent or other perpetrator about the abuse. Both the anger and the confrontation are meant to heal the victim, not to blame the abuser, and are vital components of recovering from sexual addiction.

Understanding abuse allows people to recognize what happened to them and to see how they cope with it through their addictions. It enables them to understand how painful the abuse was, how frightened they were, how alone they felt, and how angry they are. Acknowledging these feelings and finding healthy ways to express and cope with them can heal them.

To be abused by a parent or family member is an intensely powerful experience. It leads to feelings that are strong, confusing, frightening, and can lead to coping strategies that may be sinful and self-destructive. People who sin and alienate themselves from God have often felt alienated from parental love. To change, they must accept that at the time of the abuse, they did the best they could—they survived. But now they can make new choices, including the choice to accept the love of a God who is not like their family members.

By confronting the abuse, the victim accepts how powerfully damaging the experience was and seeks to stop the behavior from happening in the future. Victims of abuse need to watch themselves so as not to repeat their families' mistakes. We all tend to reenact what we learned in childhood. No matter how abusive the family behaviors were, what we grew up with was what we considered "normal"—and we may repeat abusive patterns without even thinking about it.

Sex addicts must look at what happened to them, understand it, allow themselves to feel the pain rather than addictively avoid it, and confront it as a sign that they know it was wrong. This is a process that may take a long time, but it is vital to making healthier choices in the future. When sex addicts make those new choices, they break the cycle of sinful abusive behavior, and then the sins of the parents won't be passed down from generation to generation.

This constructive awareness does, in fact, honor our families in the way God commands. When Nathan confronted David about his adulterous relationship with Bathsheba, he honored David enough to seek his restoration. When sex addicts hold family members accountable, they also honor them by seeking restoration and reconciliation. Restoration can only take place when past behaviors aren't repeated and feelings are expressed and openly discussed.

TYPES OF ABUSE

When identifying family wounds and abuse, it is important to consider four areas of human experience: emotional, physical, sexual, and spiritual. There are two kinds of abuse: invasion and abandonment. If the boundaries in a family have become too loose, emotional, physical, sexual, or spiritual boundaries are crossed. This is an invasion. If the boundaries in a family have become too rigid, family members do not get the love, attention, nurturing, or information they need to thrive. This is abandonment.

In his research with 1,000 sex addicts, Pat Carnes found that 97 percent were emotionally abused, 74 percent were physically abused, and 81 percent were sexually abused.[1] These figures reveal that abuse plays an important part in the development of sexual addiction. For sex addicts to be healed, it is vital they understand the abuse they suffered and how it has affected them.

The following chart (figure 5) provides an overview of the eight types of abuse described in this chapter. The two kinds of abuse—invasion and abandonment—are listed in the far left column. The four areas

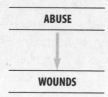

ABUSE

WOUNDS

INVASION
Boundaries are loose

Emotional	Physical	Sexual	Spiritual
• Yelling • Screaming • Put-downs • Name-calling • Profanity • Mind rape • Incest	• Hitting • Slapping • Pushing • Shoving • Spanking	• Touching or penetrating genital area • Teasing about body • Sexual humor • Sexual misinformation	• Punitive and angry messages about God • Self-righteousness • Negative messages about sex • Modeling unhealthy lifestyles

ABANDONMENT
Boundaries are rigid

Emotional	Physical	Sexual	Spiritual
• No listening • No caring or nurturing • No expression of affection	• Being left alone • Inadequate food, shelter, or clothing • No modeling of appropriate physical self-care	• Intimacy is not modeled • Lack of appropriate sexual information	• Failure to model healthy spirituality • Lack of spiritual discipline

Figure 5: Abuse

of human experience—emotional, physical, sexual, and spiritual—form the four columns. The chart demonstrates how a person could be abused invasively in emotional, physical, sexual, or spiritual ways. Likewise, persons could also be abandoned in emotional, physical, sexual, or spiritual ways. As you read through the chapter, you might want to make your own chart on a piece of paper and write down in any box the ways that you may have experienced that type of abuse.

Before reading the rest of the chapter, I encourage you to pause for a moment and pray. Ask the Holy Spirit to help you understand and accept any painful life experiences from which you need healing. Ask God for protection and strength as you reflect on family wounds and possible abuse. As you read and consider your own life, understand that you are not "digging" for experiences. The purpose of reflecting on past experiences is not to create memories of things that didn't happen. At every point, be gentle with yourself. Stop and take a break if you need to. Bottom line, talk to someone if your pain begins to feel overwhelming.

Emotional Abuse

A person's emotional boundaries can be invaded in several ways. One way is by being told they are innately "bad." Perhaps the most obvious way is the yelling and screaming that carries with it the direct verbal message: "You're no good. I hate you. You'll never amount to anything. I regret the day you were born. You're dumb, and you're ugly."

The same messages can be conveyed in a matter-of-fact way: "It doesn't surprise me that you failed, you've always failed. You might as well not apply to that college, you're not smart enough to get in. You wouldn't dare ask her out, she would never go out with someone like you."

At other times the message is very subtle: "Why didn't you get better grades? Your brother always did. Why are you dating that guy? He's a real loser." Some of us are familiar with a look from our parents, a frown, a slump of the shoulders, a pointing of the finger, a tone of the voice, or a sigh of despair.

All of these messages are abusive. They are the result of misplaced anger inappropriately expressed and not intended for constructive criticism or discipline. They are abusive because they create long-lasting and damaging wounds in the victim.

The second way people can be emotionally invaded is to be convinced their thoughts and feelings are "bad." "Mind rape" is a rather harsh but appropriate description of this kind of abuse in which a person is not allowed to have his or her feelings. A statements such as, "Please don't feel that way," or anger statements like, "That's a stupid way to feel," or "Cheer up and get your act together," are examples of mind rape. Family members are encouraged to suppress feelings in order to help someone else: "It hurts me when you're sad," or "You frighten me when you're angry," or "I worry when you worry," or "If Dad knew you felt that way, he'd die."

Another common message is, "You don't need to feel that way." This kind of mind rape is based on minimizing and is often accompanied with reasons why the victim doesn't need to feel that way. Solutions may even be offered: "You don't need to feel that way because you could do this to solve your problem." When family members are tempted to be happy, proud, or excited, they might be encouraged to suppress even these positive feelings as a way to avoid conceit. They might also feel lonely because no one else in the family knows how to experience these feelings.

Mind rape can occur when people are convinced they are not mature for feeling the way they do. One of the earliest messages many of us receive is, "Big girls/boys don't cry." Along the way we may be encouraged to "grow up," "act your age," or "stop being a baby."

Christians add mini-sermons to their messages with the theme, "A mature Christian wouldn't feel that way." We might be convinced our salvation is not intact if we feel sad, anxious, or angry. At my grandmother's funeral, the minister convinced us all to stop crying as a way to reflect our Christian belief in Grandma's salvation. While I believe I will indeed see her again, telling us not to cry at her funeral robbed us of our ability to grieve. I call this "religious mind rape."

In mind rape, the content of the message is often correct, but the timing is inappropriate and is designed to stop people from feeling. The intentions may be loving, but the "mind rapist" is uncomfortable or inept with emotions and avoids that discomfort by stopping someone else from having them.

Mind rape occurs when someone does not listen to or accept the validity of someone else's feelings. The result is that the victim begins to think it is bad, immature, irresponsible, weak, unfaithful, or otherwise unacceptable to have those feelings. But somewhere inside these feelings remain buried.

Later on in life, victims of mind rape may have similar feelings to the ones suppressed when they were younger. As a result, they continue to hide their feelings and to look for ways to numb or escape them altogether, while at the same time condemning themselves for not being able to feel. To the outsider, abuse victims seem to hide their feelings intentionally. That is not the case. Abuse victims are either too numb, too afraid, or too ashamed to talk about feelings. They think, "If you really knew me, you would hate me." They have an extremely hard time being honest with their feelings.

A third kind of invasive emotional abuse occurs when a parent creates a marriage-like relationship with a child. The lonely parent may have a bad marriage or be a single parent, and turns to the child as a special friend, buddy, confidant, and companion. The child learns to listen to, accompany, and nurture the parent. What the parent likes, the child likes. What the parent does, the child does. This is called covert emotional incest.[2]

This may seem like a very special relationship, for the child gets to do privileged things with one of his or her parents. He or she may feel extremely powerful because even at a young age the parent is sharing feelings with the child that are not shared with anyone else.

However, the child's feelings, needs, interests, and abilities are not attended to. If Dad wants him to be a baseball player, that's what he'll be. If Mom wants her to go to law school, that's what she'll do. The result? Victims lose touch with who they are and what they like. Their identities are made up of what their parents think, like, and feel.

One man told me about his girlfriend, who called her mother constantly, spent excessive amounts of time with her, and even oriented some of their dates around her. "Do you think I should marry this woman?" he asked me.

"No," I replied. "It would be a case of bigamy. She's already married to her mother."

Emotional incest can exist between a father and son, father and daughter (Daddy's little girl), mother and son, or mother and daughter. The other parent is excluded from the relationship, sometimes in obvious ways ("Your father's never home") and sometimes in less obvious ways ("Why don't just you and I go to the game? Mom doesn't like baseball anyway"). The message is clear. The other parent has some negative characteristic that makes it imperative that the incestuous parent and child "stick together."

People who are victims of emotional incest grow up with a voice inside them that always wonders, "What would Mom/Dad think about this?" They don't know how to nurture, like, or care for themselves, but they do know how to take care of Mom or Dad. As they become adults they may turn this need to care for one parent into a need to care for others. Just as their identities as children were formed by how well they took care of their parent, their identities as adults may be formed by how well they can take care of others.

Over the years of my work in the field of sexual addiction, I have noticed how many pastors, counselors, and other caregiving professionals are victims of emotional incest. They learned how to care for others and went into professions that allow them to continue doing so. The problem is not that they may not be legitimately called into these professions. God can use our brokenness to be wonderful healers. The problem occurs when these people know only how to care for others and have no idea how to care for themselves. This imbalance leads to what is often called "burnout." It is tiring, stressful, angering, and sad to always give and never allow oneself to receive.

The opposite of invasive emotional abuse is emotional abandonment. This type of abuse is just as devastating. Victims of abandonment have experienced someone leaving them emotionally. This person may be physically present, but they don't talk, share themselves, or listen to the family member needing emotional nurturing. They seem cold, distant, or unconcerned.

If this family member does care, he or she is not able to express it, and family members are held at arm's length. Parents and others who perpetrate this type of abuse may also be abuse victims and think no one needs their emotional care. Whatever the case, they don't know how to give of themselves in an emotionally nurturing way and their children feel abandoned.

In the emotional incest described earlier, the parent who commits incest usually forms an alliance with the child against the other parent.

If the other parent does nothing to prevent this or even goes along with it, this is abandonment. The very same child can be abandoned by one parent and emotionally abused by the other.

When a young child is emotionally abandoned, a very deep emotional void is created. The child may not be consciously aware of it but does know a profound loneliness and longing for affection. The child may have this feeling even when many people are around and trying to offer affection. However, the love and nurture of a parent can never be replaced, and nothing can fill that void. Sexual addiction may be an attempt to find love and nurturing care, but it is a misplaced search and never works.

Physical Abuse

Invasive physical abuse occurs when a person's body is hit, slapped, shoved, or pushed, or when some other form of physical violence takes place. Children, spouses, even grandparents, are likely to be victims of physical harm at the hands of a family member. Physical abuse occurs when one person is angry and tries to control another. Spanking done in anger and not for the purpose of discipline can be physically abusive. There are some experts who consider all spanking abusive. Victims of physical abuse are continually frightened and feel they don't have control of their physical safety.

Family members who witness violence can also be victims. If children see their mother being physically abused by their father, the effects can be just as damaging as if the children were also hit. Many Vietnam veterans who were not physically injured or who never injured others still experience many symptoms of chronic anxiety and depression.

This condition is called Post Traumatic Stress Disorder (PTSD). People with PTSD learn how to "dissociate" their minds and emotions from the reality around them. Their minds leave their bodies and go someplace else, to other thoughts or safe imaginary places. Certain behaviors or chemicals may be used to dissociate and thereby become the seeds of addiction. Many sex addicts who were physically abused suffer from PTSD.

Physical abandonment abuse occurs when basic physical needs are not met. Inadequate shelter, food, clothing, and medical care are not provided. A more subtle form of physical abandonment occurs when children are not taught to take care of themselves physically. Children need to learn how to go to bed on time, eat nutritious foods, brush their teeth, take care of personal hygiene, and exercise. When self-care is not modeled or taught, abandonment takes place.

Physical abandonment may also take place when a child is left alone, particularly when very small. The child may develop a sense of not being physically safe even though no physical danger is present. When both parents choose to work outside the home, possibly leaving a child to care for himself, the child may feel physically abandoned.

Sexual Abuse

Estimates vary greatly, but it is believed that 25 to 33 percent of all women have at some time in their lives been sexually abused. While we used to assume it was rare for a man to have been sexually abused, we now believe 10 to 15 percent of men have been abused in this way. How can we have accurate figures about this problem when it is such a difficult one to admit? Sexual abuse is such a damaging problem that many people repress the ugliness of the experience, don't remember it, and might even deny they are victims.

Invasive sexual abuse involves having the genital areas touched or penetrated by someone who holds either physical or emotional power over the victim. As a result, victims lose the sense that they have control of their bodies and live in perpetual fear of being "invaded" or of something harmful happening. Like physical abuse victims, they may also suffer the symptoms of Post Traumatic Stress Disorder. As adults they may have great difficulty with normal sexual activity. Many may not remember the childhood experience and do not even know what's wrong with them. This can cause great shame and confusion. "What's wrong with me? Why am I so afraid? Why can't I be normal sexually?" Many people, in fact, ask these questions even if they do remember the sexual abuse.

Often the sexual abuser is a trusted person. As a result, the victim may have difficulty trusting. If the abuser was a man, men may not be trusted. If a female abuser is involved, women will not be trusted. If the abuser was a professional, authority may not be respected. If the abuser was a pastor, God himself might not be trusted.

There are more subtle forms of invasive sexual abuse. Kissing, hugging, touching, lap sitting, and tickling may have the same effect as more direct sexual abuse. The victim will have a sense that the physical contact is not for the purpose of healthy nurturing but rather for the sexual gratification of the other person.

Many children have at one time or another slept in the same bedroom or even the same bed with a parent. Sometimes it is because the child was frightened by the dark or a thunderstorm. But it may be that the parent is emotionally or sexually lonely. It is not necessarily wrong for a child to occasionally sleep in the parents' bedroom. The distinction centers on why the child is there. If the child feels uncomfortable with it, it is abusive.

A parent may walk into the bedroom or the bathroom when a child is getting dressed, bathing, or using the bathroom for its normally intended purpose. When the child enters adolescence, this becomes abusive, even if it involves the parent of the same sex, because it teaches children they have no control over their environment or their privacy. Feelings of shame or embarrassment result. Later in life they may become protective and unable to experience their body without those feelings of shame.

Another form of invasive abuse occurs when children are teased about their body, their development, or any sexual or romantic feelings they have. A woman told me that her father announced at a Thanksgiving gathering of her entire family that she had started menstruating. He kidded her that she needed to start watching out for boys and it was his job to protect her. This amazingly insensitive comment had more to do with the father's discomfort with sex than it did with his fear of boys in his daughter's life, and he passed that discomfort on to his daughter. It was abusive. It created wounds. The woman telling me the story had tears in her eyes, and she was seventy years old.

Our families are bad enough; our peers can be worse. As adolescents and teens, many people were teased mercilessly about their bodies by their "friends." This teasing is extremely painful and also reflects incorrect sexual information.

Our entire culture sexually abuses us through the messages it sends to us on TV, movies, radio, or magazines. We innocently take in misinformation while we wait to pay for our groceries. I am often in airports and usually buy a paper to read on the plane. Just walking into an airport bookstore one is assaulted with blatant sexual images on the covers of many magazines. I didn't invite those images into my life and am forced to deal with them. I find that on a daily basis, I must continually seek God's view of healthy sexuality as opposed to what the world promotes.

The other side of invasive sexual abuse is abandonment sexual abuse. Ask yourself, What messages would you receive about sex if your family never talked about it? Would it be hard for you to imagine, biologically, how you even got here if your parents never touched each other, seemed affectionate, or mentioned the word *sex*? Would you feel afraid about your physical and sexual development if you had no one to talk to? For example, junior high students take a shower after physical education. Do you remember that first shower, and being naked in front of your peers? Instead of physical education this experience becomes a class in comparative anatomy. Whom did you talk to about whatever feelings you had?

The effect of this abandonment is that people grow up believing such feelings are unique to them. Since no one else has ever talked to them about normal sexual feelings they assume their sexual feelings are abnormal. They may even start to interpret their normal sexual curiosity as perverted if they can't compare it to others' and discover it is normal. They may become afraid of their sexual feelings. They might infer that since sex is never talked about, it must be bad. Sex addicts have extremely distorted and fearful ideas about sexuality. They don't think they can talk to anyone about it. Abandonment sexual abuse prevents the adult sex addict from getting desperately needed help.

Spiritual Abuse

We were having coffee at the home of some Christian friends when their three-year-old daughter, who was playing on the staircase banister, fell off, bumped her head, and began to cry. The mother put her arms around her and said, "There now, big girls don't cry." Then she said, "I wonder if Jesus wanted you sliding down that banister? I think that if he did he wouldn't have let you bump your head."

Often parents discipline their children by warning them of the consequences that God might send. It may be theologically correct to teach the consequences of sinful behavior, but there is a way to do so that emphasizes the love of God rather than the wrath of God. Would a wrathful God have sent his Son to die for us? Yet Christians of many different denominations have been raised with an image of a strict and vengeful God.

Invasive spiritual abuse convinces people they are evil and do only sinful things, making them so afraid of God's anger and disapproval that they look for rigid, black-and-white answers. Without the right answers, they won't do the right things, and God will be angry. People subject to this kind of abuse also make sure they read the Bible and pray—not to nurture themselves spiritually, but to appease God and avoid punishment. They may also learn to repress feelings that they have been taught are "un-Christian," such as anger or fear. This form of abuse is what I call "religious mind rape."

Invasive spiritual abuse might also teach us very negative attitudes about sexuality. Instead of celebrating God's great gift of marital sexuality, we might have learned that sex is dirty, disgusting, awful, or only for the purpose of procreation and not to be enjoyed. The silence of the church about sexual issues contributes to the feeling that sex must be bad if the church doesn't talk about it.

We must be careful not to separate the body from the soul. This is called "dualism." Dualism posits that the soul is good, but the body is bad. To really develop the soul, a person should deny the appetites of the body. When sex is not talked about in healthy ways, as God intends, it leaves us with fearful attitudes about sexual desires.

This fear of sex affects sex addicts in two ways. First, it encourages them to keep quiet about their problem. If they have committed sexual sins and know the church has negative and judgmental attitudes about sexuality, they will be even more ashamed. Sexual sinners should feel guilty and make amends for what they have done, but an overwhelming sense of personal shame and a fear that God or the church will punish them may lead them to be totally silent. As a result, they may never get help.

Second, negative attitudes about sex make it a tantalizing "forbidden fruit." This makes the pursuit of sex a dangerous and therefore even more stimulating activity. Sex becomes exciting for both its pleasure and its danger. These qualities can be addicting because they provide escape from feelings.

Remember that to many sex addicts, "for sex to be good, it has to be bad."[3] For sex to be exciting or pleasurable, it has to be forbidden. Often, sex addicts are attracted to "bad" sex because of their family background. If they have been sexually abused and at the same time told not to be promiscuous or to avoid sex, they are taught that sex is hurtful and emotionally painful. A child in this situation may think, "Dad tells me not to be sexual, but he does have sex with me. That really hurts, but it must be all right since it is Dad doing it." This child is programmed to look for painful sexual relationships later in life.

These dynamics also condition a person to be rebellious about sex. "My parents say I shouldn't. My church says I shouldn't. Yet they have abused or abandoned me. I'm angry. What does God care? I'm going to be sexual anyway." Whether verbalized or unconscious, this thought has the power to lead a person into rebellious sexual encounters.

My own informal research confirms what other sociologists of religion suggest: People from rigidly religious homes that teach negative messages about sex are more likely to have difficulty with sexual addiction. Several prostitutes have told me they are glad to see Christian conventions come to town because their business increases. Hotel chains report that in-room use of televised pornography increases during Christian conventions. And I have consulted with evangelical churches in which affairs in the congregation were rampant, and one in which wife swapping was common among members of an adult Sunday school class.

In the spiritual abuse of abandonment, no one provides modeling or teaching about healthy spirituality. Such parents may be pillars of the church and pay lip service to Christian values but not live them out at home. They may push church attendance and religious practices on the child without taking them seriously themselves. Worse, they may preach religious values but violate them, even going so far as to commit other forms of abuse. This hypocrisy destroys trust. When people are abandoned spiritually, they do not have resources to turn to when they get into trouble. Many sex addicts are completely devoid of a healthy sense of spirituality and are alienated from the church because of all the fear and negativity described above. A major challenge of recovery for them is to develop a healthy sense of spirituality.

Cultural Abuse

Since this book was first published in 1992, I have worked with many sexually addicted clients who came from families that didn't abuse in the ways just described. Abuse happens beyond the home as well. It is not just families who are to blame. We live in a culture that is increasingly violent, both physically and sexually. For example, when I turn on a football game, I don't invite sexual images into my life but they will be there. When I go into a bookstore, I don't invite all those magazine covers that depict the same kind of nudity that would have been inside pornographic magazines years ago. The same could be said of many forms of popular culture.

Today, we know that even children can be accidentally exposed to graphic sexuality and violence on the Internet. There is an epidemic of children becoming addicted to pornography and masturbation as a result. A therapist recently called me and reported the case of an eight-year-old girl who couldn't stop looking at Internet pornography. Her family was a relatively stable one, but she had stumbled across this material by herself. The fact that it was there for her to see is evidence of an abusive culture.

THE WOUNDED SELF AND SHAME

When children are abused, they are wounded emotionally, sexually, spiritually, and sometimes physically (see figure 6). They are too small and too helpless to defend themselves against these injuries. What are children to think about themselves when they are being invaded or abandoned? They come to a very logical conclusion: "If this is happening to me, I must be bad, because bad people are punished." Or, "If no one loves me, it must be because I am bad. Good people are loved."

These wounds lead to a very deep feeling called "shame." There are both unhealthy and healthy experiences of shame. As John Bradshaw points out in his book *Healing the Shame that Binds You*, shame in itself is not bad.[4] Healthy shame recognizes that all people have both abilities and limitations. Healthy shame teaches us that we need others, that we can't exist on our own and always take care of ourselves. It is part of the human condition and points a person toward a healthy dependence on others and on God.

Abuse victims, however, have internalized this sense of shame and believe themselves to be completely worthless. Healthy shame expresses the conviction that human beings are not able to earn their own salvation and that they must depend on God. Unhealthy shame tells people to believe they do not deserve God's salvation and probably won't be able to accept it. This kind of shame convinces people they have an evil nature and there is no goodness inside.

Shame is not the same thing as guilt. Dr. Sandra Wilson, author of several books on codependency and shame, gives the best distinction: "Guilt is when we know we've made mistakes. Shame is when we feel we are a mistake."[5]

Unhealthy shame prevents people from giving themselves any kind of affirmation. Nothing they do, no victories won, no accomplishments of any kind, convince them they are good. They may go to church and hear the Word of God, they may believe in Christ, they may know him in their head, but they don't feel him in their heart.

Unhealthy shame is the central feeling of the abused and wounded child. Attached to this core feeling are other feelings (see figure 6 on the next page). The abandoned child feels lonely and sad. The abused child feels anxious and fearful.

Another feeling attached to shame is anger. Although abuse victims believe they deserved the abuse, another part of them is deeply angry about the abuse. Yet they don't allow themselves to feel, much less experience, this anger. It lies buried and festers, and sometimes reveals itself in addictive behavior. The anger leaks out somehow no matter how hard a person tries to repress it.

I have always been fascinated with how Christian sex addicts justify committing sexual sin. One obvious answer is that sin, of any kind, is rebellious and angry. Sex addicts can even be angry with God, thinking, "How could God let this happen to me?" Since God did not prevent abuse, this anger can lead a sex addict to think, "I don't care what God thinks. He didn't help me. I'm going to help myself."

When children and adolescents are abused, they are logical enough to think, "If I were a good person, this wouldn't be happening," or "If I were a good person, I would get my needs met." The logical conclusion is that I must be a bad and worthless person.

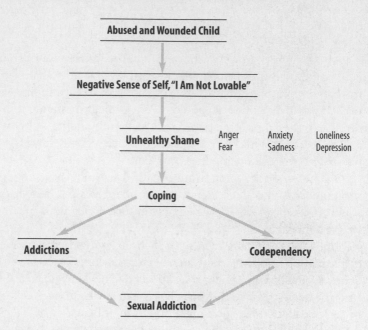

Figure 6: Abused and Wounded Child

This kind of sad, despairing, angry, rebellious, and (perhaps) logical thinking leads sex addicts to four core beliefs about themselves:

1. I am a bad, unworthy person.
2. No one will love me as I am.
3. No one can take care of my needs but me.
4. Sex is my most important need.[6]

Sex addicts believe that sexual activity is the only way to meet their needs for love and nurturing. For many of them, sex was the only way they received attention (of any kind) and physical touch. They learned to make the connection between love, nurture, touch, and sex. Sex became their most important need because it was the only association they had between having needs and having them met. How do sex addicts cope with their deep needs for love and their deep sense of shame? That is the topic of the next chapter.

CHAPTER 7

HOW SEX ADDICTS COPE
WITH ABUSE

Sex addicts come from families in which the dynamics are mostly unhealthy and abusive. The abuse has led them to feel shame in unhealthy ways. Their parents and other family members have modeled many of the self-destructive strategies addicts use to cope with abuse and shame.

The strategies sex addicts employ for dealing with abuse and shame can be divided into two very broad categories—escape and codependency. First, they try to escape feelings of unhealthy shame. Next, they seek to gain from others the approval they can't give themselves and thereby become codependent.

ESCAPE

Because sex addicts can't tolerate painful feelings, they seek to escape the feelings through sexual activity. Research has shown that sexual activity and sexual fantasy can alter brain chemistry and produce profound feelings of pleasure.[1] This can be a beautiful experience between two committed people. Sex addicts, however, are in the business of altering their brain chemistry, and thereby their mood, all the time. They use sex like a drug to produce a high. As the disease progresses, the sex addict cares less and less who the sexual partner is. The main pursuit is the high. If they can't find a partner, masturbation gives them a quick fix.

Sometimes the danger inherent in promiscuous sexual activity produces adrenaline that can also be addicting. Sex addicts may pursue dangerous sexual liaisons, such as men who have sex with married women whose husbands are due home shortly. They get a high from the sex, from a new partner, and from the danger. In their excitement, they temporarily forget their anxieties, fears, sadness, loneliness, or anger.

Sexual activity is not the only addiction sex addicts might use to escape. Addictions of all kinds can come into play. Any of them can be dangerously pursued and are therefore exciting, giving addicts a rush of adrenaline.

The more profoundly abused a person has been, the greater the likelihood of multiple addictions. For example, roughly 50 percent of all sex addicts are also alcoholics.[2] A sex addict may need to be in recovery from addictions to alcohol, drugs, and other substances or behaviors.

Escape and mood alteration are not the only reasons certain chemicals or behaviors, like sex, become addictive. Another possibility is that they are used as a reward. Sex addicts believe that no one else is going to take care of them, so when they feel they have been good or done something well, they reward themselves with many other addictive things: a cigarette, a drink, a shopping trip, or a joint.

CODEPENDENCY

The other route to dealing with unhealthy shame is to find approval outside of the self. A shamed person doesn't like herself and must find someone who does.

Betty grew up in a very strict home. Her parents were often critical. She never dated in high school and thought no one would ever like her. She was amazed Harry even asked her out when she got to college. They had a stormy relationship in which Harry often was critical. Although it hurt her, Betty often agreed with his criticisms and felt she did have a lot to improve. Betty married Harry right after college. They both drank some in college but thought they would "grow out of it." Betty did, but Harry didn't. He continued to drink. Over time the drinking got worse. He lost several jobs because of it. When he was drunk, Harry would often rage at the whole family. Many mornings Harry was unable to go into work, and Betty would call his boss saying Harry was sick. More and more, Betty found herself going into chat rooms on the Internet. She met many people, including men who praised and affirmed her. One of these relationships progressed to talking on the phone, then to talking about sex, and finally to an affair. Betty eventually stopped the affair, afraid that Harry would find out, but found herself going right back to the chat rooms.

Betty's codependency with Harry kept her lonely and ashamed. She found approval on the Internet and this habit is gradually leading her down the path of sexual addiction. Codependency is an addiction to approval and to any person whose approval is sought. It is anything done to obtain, maintain, and manipulate a person's approval. Sex addicts believe one way to get approval is through sexual activity. They might think that people willing to be sexual with them must like them. If sex addicts are to heal, they must learn how to find approval in healthy ways. It is vital then to fully understand codependency.

Codependency was originally used to describe the condition of people in a significant relationship with an alcoholic. The alcoholic is dependent on alcohol, and the codependent is dependent on the alcoholic. A codependent's attachment to and need for approval is so uncontrollable that she can't leave or take care of herself despite the drinking and abusive behaviors that go along with alcoholism.

Codependency is often used to describe anyone addicted to another person. Most codependents were abandoned as children and grow up to be deathly afraid of someone leaving them again. They will completely sacrifice their needs and interests if that is what it takes to please the people whose approval they so desperately need. This sacrifice brings with it a great cost. Codependents work so hard to get others to like them, they burn themselves out and get tired and depressed. They are so afraid of someone leaving that they develop great anxieties. Preoccupied with what they can do to maintain another's approval, they neglect other important matters in life.

Codependents may believe that people will like them if they have enough money, a nice house, a fancy car, a powerful job, or the right educational degrees. Some ministers are "ordained codependents," believing people will like them only if they are ministers. Codependents busy themselves, sometimes feverishly, to try to get ahead in life. Sometimes success gives them short bursts of approval and they feel good for a brief time, but it doesn't last. Then they need another fix and get busy again to earn it.

Codependents use many ways to try to keep a person with them. Sometimes they don't need the person to like them so much as they simply need them to be there. They might do countless acts of service, sacrificing their own time and interests, to please another. They can be endless caretakers.

Sex addicts who are codependents need a lot of sex to like themselves. They think sex is their most important need. Through sex, they get the admiration and nurture they are starved for. They might employ codependent strategies not only to keep a person with them, but also to get sex from them.

To all of Helen's friends, her husband, Henry, seemed like the model man. He was always doing things for her, buying her things, bringing her flowers, and helping with household chores. Her time was his time. What she wanted he wanted. Henry was such a great husband, how could she refuse him sexually? She was shocked one day when she found a stack of pornography in his closet. Henry was a codependent sex addict continually trying to earn sexual favors from his wife.

Although they may bring temporary relief from the pain and anxieties of being abandoned, codependent strategies seldom work for long. Usually codependency compels a person to pursue sexual activities that are sinful and thereby shameful. Codependency temporarily relieves shame but in the long term it only serves to increase it. Many people go back and forth between a desperate search for approval and a need to escape the feeling they never really get approval. It is an endless, vicious cycle.

Sexual addiction is an attempt to manage shame by employing the strategies of escape and codependency simultaneously. Sexual activity becomes both an escape and a search for approval at the same time.

Now consider the overall impact of the dynamics discussed in this section (see figure 7). Sexual addiction is powerful because it attempts to manage the unhealthy sense of shame that an unhealthy family has created.

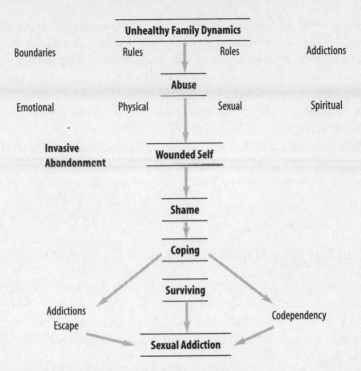

Figure 7: The Family of Origin Roots of Sexual Addiction

Sex is an attractive activity to the addict, not just because it is a tool the devil uses to lead people astray, but also because it can be used to medicate the wounds of childhood. As such it is a survival strategy. This strategy avoids short-term pain for a slower death. Just as a cocaine addict longs for the medication of the next high, a sex addict longs for the medication of the next sexual activity.

Anyone who has ever been frustrated with a sex addict because he or she wouldn't stop acting out needs to remember that sexual activity, at least in the mind of addicts, has allowed them to survive pain. It is not that sex addicts don't want to give up sex. It is not that they are terrible, sinful, immoral people. It is because they can't give up the coping strategies they believe have kept them alive for years.

When a spouse, a friend, a pastor, or a counselor asks a sex addict to stop acting out sexually, the sex addict hears this message at one level and agrees with it. Yet there is a simultaneous voice inside that says, "If I give this up, I will die. The pain is too intense. I can't stand it." Another voice, at another level, quickly follows: "Why should I give this up? It is the only thing that I do for myself. No one else takes care of me." This last voice is the voice of the abandonment victim and says, often in anger, "Don't tell me to stop. People have been denying me my needs for years. Who will take care of me?"

When we seek to help a sex addict stop, we are dealing with an adult who agrees with us and a wounded child who does not. If our logic and strategies are aimed only at the adult who agrees with us already, we will fail.

RELIGIOUS ADDICTION AND CODEPENDENCY

When Dan was a boy his parents made him go to church so he could avoid going to hell. Dan was emotionally abused by his dad, who never affirmed anything he did. Although Dan's successful law practice brought him praise, he didn't enjoy it and didn't like himself. He turned to visiting prostitutes more and more.

Dan was also a pillar in his church. He served on many committees, and, as president of the church council, he attended almost every function. He also taught Sunday school and sang in the choir. The pastor called him his "right-hand man" and didn't know what he would do without Dan.

Yet when I talked to Dan he confessed he never felt satisfied and always felt guilty. He looked constantly for more religious activity to help him feel better. He told me he had decided to quit his law practice and go to seminary at age forty-three. Maybe becoming a pastor would satisfy him.

Dan did go to seminary, but he was arrested for soliciting prostitution. Eventually, he went to treatment and returned to his law practice, where he works primarily with sex offenders. He discovered that he was called to ministry not by God but by his guilt and religious addiction.

Religious addiction involves the notion that there is a formula that leads to approval, happiness, and success. Sex addicts believe that if they can get the formula right, their lust will be taken away.

The danger of religious addiction is that the effort or the practice of religion becomes more important than any hoped-for result. Being religiously busy becomes more important than an intimate and nurturing relationship with God. Sex addicts have been impaired in their families and do not know how to have healthy intimacy. How can they know intimacy with a God who is called Father when they have not learned healthy intimacy in other relationships?

Jesus encountered religious addiction. In Mark 2:23–28 incredulous Pharisees question him about his disciples breaking ceremonial law by plucking ears of grain on the Sabbath. Jesus reminds them of how King David ate bread from the high altar, which, lawfully, was meant only for the priests. Jesus goes on to point out that the Sabbath was made for people, not people for the Sabbath. We do not obey laws in order to please and pacify God. Rather, laws are made for our protection and to teach us how to nurture ourselves and have a healthy relationship with God and others.

The Pharisees were religiously addicted. The practice of religion was more important to them than people and their spiritual needs. The rigidity of their religiously addicted thinking prevented the Pharisees from experiencing Jesus as the Messiah.

Religious addiction occurs when we, like the Pharisees, use repetitive religious behaviors to get the formula right in order to feel happy, escape our feelings, and avoid intimacy. Religious addicts think if they read the Bible one hour a day, two hours would be better. If they go to church twice a week, three times would be more productive. Memorizing a hundred Scripture verses is not as good as a thousand. Serving on one committee is not as good as on five.

Religiously addicted persons create a false sense of security. They believe that the more they do, the better God will like them. In most churches, they also get lots of affirmation for their hard work and extreme effort.

Religious addiction becomes a religious workaholism. The work, in itself, becomes an escape. Work takes lots of thought and energy. It creates its own excitement and adrenaline, which distracts the addict from other feelings, however painful. The amount of work may even create great things, like new church buildings, higher budgets, or more members. There is an excitement to the fruits of this labor. Yet, for sex addicts, it is merely another escape.

Since the fix is only a temporary one, more and more religious activity is needed in order to maintain it. This is the tolerance factor. More and more of the same behavior is needed to sustain the high. Many religious addicts burn themselves out, perhaps even leaving the church to escape their endless cycle of activity. If they don't leave, they might stay around and become resentful that they are the only ones who ever seem to do anything.

Ultimately, religious addicts become depressed that their activity hasn't produced the happiness they thought it would. Sex addicts don't achieve freedom from their lust and sexual behaviors and can become very disillusioned with God and religion. I know countless numbers of sex addicts who have left the church for these reasons.

Work and the excitement and adrenaline of it are one form of escape for a religious addict. This achieves the effect of avoiding pain. There are also religious ways to alter mood. Mood-altering experiences are not unique to cults or Eastern religions. The music, the rituals, the repetitive prayers or readings, and the somber or celebrative atmospheres of church may have a mood-altering effect. Christians might say, "They are supposed to make us feel better and help us to be closer to God." However, an addict does not use them for relationship, but to alter mood and avoid relationship. To a religious addict, worship can be an ecstatic experience in which they get "carried away." They get carried away from a relationship with God, not toward it.

These forms of religious expression are not addictive in themselves. Religious addicts allow the jubilance or the soothing nature of certain religious styles to create what is, in effect, a trancelike state, in order to help them avoid what they feel. It is much the same as putting music in your stereo not as an expression of how you feel but as a way of altering how you are feeling. You may feel lousy, so you put on happy or joyous music to make you feel differently. This isn't bad in itself, but if done all the time to always avoid feelings, it could be addictive. Remember, something can be addictive if it is done repetitively for the purpose of avoiding feelings.

When the formula is working right, the religious addict indeed begins to feel "good." However, this feeling shouldn't be confused with a genuine experience of peace. It is not that. The addict's good feeling is based on temporarily avoiding the truly painful feelings inside.

Sex addicts crave this experience of being and feeling good. Religious addiction serves as a form of escape. In spite of the terribly sinful things they are doing, they can have a temporary fix of feeling like they are not sinful but rather spiritual people.

An interesting feature of religious addiction is that it causes others in the church to think religious addicts are actually very spiritual people. If sex addicts are also religious addicts, they may seem wonderfully devout to those who don't really know them. If their sexual sinfulness becomes public, it will surprise those same people because it seems so out of character. Christians may ask, "How could she have done those things?" They may find themselves becoming angry with the "hypocrite." What they are actually experiencing is a challenge to their faith. If people have committed sexual sin themselves, discovering it in others makes them uncomfortable, for it reminds them of what they have done. It is easier to blame the sex addict and avoid them than it is to look at one's own sexual sins. Often, when people reject and judge a sex addict's sinful behavior, they are also guilty of sexual addiction.

In combination with religious addiction, codependency can lead a sex addict into a maddening pace of activity and caregiving work. This is one reason why so many codependents, who are religiously and sexually addicted, are perceived as pillars of the church and shining examples of faith.

Sex addict codependents have heard the commandment, "Love your neighbor" (Leviticus 19:18). But they never seem to have heard the second part of the passage, "as yourself," for they do not know how to love themselves. Codependents in the church have retranslated this verse into: "Love others because you want them to love you." However, since sex addicts don't love themselves, they are unable to love others. Instead of loving others, they do things for others hoping that others will love them. Others must love them because they can't love themselves.

Christian charity work done as the result of codependent thinking is not done in response to God's love as it should be; rather, it is an attempt to earn God's love. Codependent thinking leads to a theology of salvation by works and not salvation by faith. The challenge to a sexually addicted codependent is to learn that he or she doesn't have to burn out trying to earn God's or anyone else's nurture. It is while we were yet sinners that Christ died for us. His love does not need to be earned or deserved—it is a gift freely offered.

Shame creates codependency and prevents many people, including sex addicts, from accepting the gift of Jesus Christ. A sexually addicted codependent thinks, "If God sent Jesus to die for sins, it wasn't for mine; they are too sexually terrible for even Jesus to imagine." When they think like this, their sexual behaviors remain the secret sin that not even Christ can heal.

The codependent needs to find approval from others. Sexual and religious addiction are attempts at dealing with shame. They are false substitutes. They provide short and temporary relief but it never lasts. The obvious questions are, What is the real solution? What brings genuine healing? How does a person find a relationship with God in Christ? How does one find peace, serenity, grace, love, nurture, passion, and acceptance? These questions lead us to the chapters in the next section, "Healing the Wounds of Sexual Addiction."

PART III

HEALING THE WOUNDS OF SEXUAL ADDICTION

CHAPTER 8

THE JOURNEY
OF HEALING

Healing is a lifetime journey, not a one-time event. This chapter is about taking the first steps on that healing journey. My hope and prayer is that it will be helpful to all, addicted or not, who seek emotional and spiritual wholeness. You may be an addict who has tried for years to get well. Or perhaps you are living with a sex addict and wonder if there is any hope. Whatever your need, I pray you find comfort and hope in the pages that follow.

Knowing there is a process, plan, and vision for healing often provides a sense of peace. The process of healing from sexual addiction includes answering important questions, creating accountability, and understanding how people change. If you are an addict who has resisted the healing journey, you may not always like the questions I ask or the advice I give. Healing is hard work and addicts and those in pain find that patience is often elusive. But I can tell you that the principles outlined here do work. They are forged out of my own journey and grounded in my experiences of companioning many others on their healing journeys.

THREE SPIRITUAL QUESTIONS

When working with new people who want to heal from sexual addiction, whether in individual counseling, a workshop, or a seminar, I ask three spiritual questions:

1. Do you want to get well?
2. What are you thirsty for?
3. Are you willing to die to yourself?

Do You Want to Get Well?

In John 5, Jesus heals a man who has been paralyzed for thirty-eight years. For all of that time he had been lying by the pool of Bethesda, which was said to have healing properties. Jesus knew about this man and it has always surprised me, given my counseling training, that the first question Jesus asks him is, "Do you want to get well?" What was Jesus thinking? Why didn't he ask the man how he got that way, or how it feels to be that way, or what could he do to help? Why else would the man be lying there? Jesus' question doesn't seem to be a very compassionate one. But Jesus is the master psychologist, and the paralyzed man's answer gives us a clue about Jesus' question. The man says, "Sir, I have no one to help me, and when I go down, someone gets in my way." I believe the man had adopted the identity of being paralyzed. Jesus knew that for the man to be healed, he had to want to change.

In my own experience of addiction, part of me wanted to be free and part of me didn't. As the apostle James says in his letter, I was a "double-minded man" (James 1:8). I questioned how I could give up these sexual sins—they were the way I coped, survived, and got my needs met. I had asked God to take them away but he hadn't, at least not the way I wanted him to—quickly and easily. Even though I was a Christian, I didn't really want to trust God and surrender my sexual sins to him.

The strategies for healing in this and subsequent chapters are not complicated. The key, however, is whether or not addicts really want to change. If they don't, no strategy, however simple, will work. The sin of pride is at the heart of this challenge. Can one really trust God to heal sexual addiction? My answer is an unequivocal "Yes!" Pride, though, is a difficult obstacle to overcome. Anyone who wants healing must get past the hurts and anger of the past in order to say yes to God. Addicts, for sure, must also know that there are alternative ways to find the love and nurture they need. This requires a lifetime of discovery, but it all starts with willingness.

Alcoholics Anonymous (AA) learned over fifty years ago that it is easier to help alcoholics when they "hit bottom," when their lives are so shattered and broken that denial, delusion, and excuses are wiped away. This was true for me. One of my favorite AA expressions is, "My own best thinking is what got me here." When addicts have no place else to turn, and when they have totally lost it, then they are more willing to turn to God, the only true answer.

What Are You Thirsty For?

Several years ago I counseled a famous person in southern California. He told me he had been sexual with over 3,000 women, including prostitutes whose services had cost him $3,000,000. He was a depressed, drug-addicted, and hopeless man. He looked at me and said, "All that sex was never enough. I always wanted more." He was obviously a sex addict. I told him I thought he was really thirsty for God and that sex does not quench spiritual thirst. I'm happy to say that today he is a Christian and living in a monogamous marriage, sexually pure. He says he is truly content with just one sexual partner—his wife—and that sex is satisfying because it is based on a spiritual love. His story reminds me of a story in the Bible.

John 4:6–26 tells of a Samaritan woman who had been married five times and currently lives with another man. She has come to a well to draw water at noon to avoid the respectable women of her town who come early in the morning. There she finds Jesus. She is lonely, frightened, and ashamed. She is looking for love and nurture and has failed to find it in a series of men. Jesus knows all of this. The woman offers to help Jesus draw water from the well, but he says to her, "Anyone who drinks of the water from this well will thirst again." Jesus offers the woman at the well "living water," the water of salvation.

Only in a relationship with Jesus Christ do we satisfy our deep spiritual and emotional thirst. All the false substitutes and idolatries of the world can never satisfy us the way faith can. In order to heal, addicts must begin to acknowledge that all of their strivings to satisfy their thirsts are abysmal failures. They must discover and embrace what they are truly thirsty for.

The idea of Christ's love being living water is difficult to grasp. It is often described as that which gives us life. Imagine a person who is dying of thirst after being in the desert. Addicts have been in a spiritual and emotional desert and are thirsty to the point of death. They have been drinking polluted water and it is not giving them life.

Many of my clients want to experience living water, the grace of God's forgiveness and salvation. Their minds, however, are like the coffee filters filled with junk that I described earlier. If the wounds of our lives have dumped shameful messages into our mental filters, anything we pour through those filters comes out looking and feeling like shame. Even the living water of Christ's love for us comes out as shame because we don't believe we deserve it. We must begin to put new messages into our filters in order to truly embrace what God promises to us. Although we can never totally eliminate the old messages from our memories, we can gradually diminish their power by daily reminding ourselves of the truth about God's love. In this way we quench our thirst.

Are You Willing to Die to Yourself?

The apostle Paul tells us we should lead lives of love, just as Jesus loved the church and gave himself up for her as a living sacrifice (Ephesians 5:1–2). Paul also says we should be "imitators of Christ," for we can never be truly like him. Christ died for us; he was willing to pay the price for our sins. As imitators of Christ, we must also learn about being willing to pay the price, to die to ourselves.

Lust is equal to normal sexual desire plus selfishness. Everything about lust is idolatrous, prideful, and arrogant. *Purity* is equal to normal sexual desire plus selflessness. The highest form of selflessness is a willingness to die for someone else. Think about it: Who or what would you be willing to die for? Most of us would readily die for our children. After the tragedy of the September 11 terrorist attacks, many Americans felt they would be willing to die for their country. In a similar way, those of us who want to be sexually pure in marriage must be willing to die for our spouses.

Willingness to heal includes being willing to die to something or for someone. This is the opposite of being selfish. Few are ever called to physically die for someone else, but if we want to heal we must be willing to die to our selfish needs and desires. It is in our dying to self that we experience Christ's power.

I am fascinated by the story of Lazarus in John 11. He and his two sisters, Mary and Martha, were close friends of Jesus. When he hears Lazarus is very sick, Jesus doesn't come right away. He doesn't come for days. In fact, it isn't until after Lazarus is dead and buried that Jesus finally comes. Mary and Martha rush out to meet Jesus and say, "If only you had come sooner, Lord, our brother would not have died." In essence they say, "Jesus, you're late!"

Even though Jesus knows he is going to bring Lazarus back to life, he is deeply moved by the grief of Lazarus's friends and loved ones. He comes to the tomb and asks that the stone covering it be rolled away. Martha objects, pointing out that since Lazarus has been dead for four days, there will certainly be an unpleasant odor. Jesus makes it clear he has allowed Lazarus to die in order to glorify God by raising him from the dead. It sounds cruel until we realize that it is only in death that we experience Christ's power. We can't experience that power until we die to ourselves, surrender control of our lives, and accept Christ's offer of salvation. If we are still in the business of trying to heal ourselves, it will be a long, painful, and futile struggle. We must surrender control to Christ.

Like Mary and Martha, addicts, spouses, and others have many "if-only" questions for Jesus: Where are you? What's the problem? Why won't you come and save me? Many sex addicts wonder why Jesus won't heal them before they destroy their lives. Jesus knows it is only admitting powerlessness and total brokenness—spiritual and emotional death—that enables us to turn to him.

When I crashed and burned, I lost virtually everything—money, jobs, and my reputation. It felt like I died. Emotional death comes when a person feels he or she has lost everything. The danger is that the experience is depressing. Alcoholics Anonymous, however, has long recognized that a person must hit bottom—where there is no place to go but up—in order to get sober. Hitting bottom means acknowledging that one's own best efforts have totally failed. This emotional death enables us to finally surrender control. However, letting go of control is not giving up. It is giving in. It requires surrendering attempts to help oneself and admitting powerlessness. It means asking for help. It is only when we are able to surrender to God that the process of transformation can begin.

CREATE ACCOUNTABILITY

Sex addicts who are willing to heal, who thirst for God, and are able to die to themselves need to be accountable in order to maintain sexual purity.

It is important to understand what accountability is and what it involves. For over seventeen years, I have studied and worked with the accountability models of several recovery and Twelve-Step fellowships. After trying to synthesize the wisdom of these sources, I believe the best demonstration of accountability principles in action is illustrated by the first four chapters of Nehemiah. It is a story of rebuilding a city that has been destroyed. As we will see, the process involved in rebuilding a destroyed city is the same process we can follow to establish accountability and rebuild lives destroyed by sexual addiction.

The process of establishing accountability includes ten components.

1. Begin in Sadness and Brokenness

In the story of Nehemiah, the Jewish people have been taken into captivity in Persia. Nehemiah, a slave, is cupbearer to King Artaxerxes. Although he is a slave, he is in proximity to power. Some of Nehemiah's relatives come to him and describe the devastation in Jerusalem. The city has been destroyed and its "gates have been burned with fire" (Nehemiah 1:3). Their report to Nehemiah is a plea for help. When Nehemiah hears the news, he is sad and broken; he weeps for days (1:4).

In the face of devastation caused by addiction, it is right and healthy to grieve our losses. If we fail to do this, we will continue to carry the pain of the past and, sooner or later, it will sabotage the healing process by driving us back to sexual addiction.

2. Confess and Repent

Nehemiah then prays a two-part prayer (Nehemiah 1:5–11). First, he confesses the sins of the Jewish people—failing to obey God's commands—and he states a willingness to repent and return home.

Grief over the pain and losses of sexual addiction leads to a willingness to confess our failure to obey God's commands.

3. Honestly Express Feelings and Needs

Nehemiah is still sad as he prepares wine and presents it to King Artaxerxes. The king asks Nehemiah about his sadness and what he needs. Nehemiah tells the king he is sad because Jerusalem, the city of his ancestors, has been destroyed. He asks permission to return to Jerusalem to rebuild it.

Nehemiah's honesty about his feelings and needs puts him in a vulnerable position. What if his sadness offends the king? What if his needs are ignored or denied? However, Nehemiah's honest expression of his emotions and needs secures precisely what he needs from the king.

Honestly expressing emotions and needs is one of the most difficult things for addicts to do. Many of us have spent lifetimes in self-destructive behaviors to avoid this very thing. In order to heal, however, we must learn to express our feelings and state our emotional and spiritual needs.

4. Practice in the Strength of Groups

The king grants Nehemiah's request. At this point in the story, however, Nehemiah is about to make a big mistake. He asks the king for letters of safe passage and plans to make a thousand-mile journey through enemy territory *alone*. Fortunately, the king is wiser; he equips Nehemiah not only with letters but also with army officers and the cavalry (Nehemiah 2:9).

I have never known a person to heal from sexual addiction alone. All of us need an army of support around us on the healing journey.

If we seek to stand alone, Satan will easily pick us off. In the movie *Gladiator*, Maximus, a Roman general who has been betrayed and sold into slavery, returns to Rome as a gladiator. The emperor is re-creating scenes from great Roman military victories. Maximus and other gladiators are led into the Coliseum to represent the barbarian horde slaughtered in the Second Fall of Carthage. Maximus knows his history and knows the onslaught to come. He rallies the men around him with these words, "Whatever comes through those gates, if we stay together, we can survive." The gladiators lock shields as they are surrounded by Roman chariots. Banding together in a cohort had been a great Roman military strategy for centuries. Despite the odds, Maximus leads the gladiators to victory.

Paul says Satan is like a lion who roars after his prey (1 Peter 5:8). Alone we will be defeated; in groups (cohorts) we can survive. Effective accountability happens only in groups. I often hear someone say, "I'm in accountability with _____." What happens if that person is gone, or sick, or too tired to talk? We need groups of people to be accountable to, lists of names and phone numbers to call when we are vulnerable to attack.

5. Take One Day at a Time

Nehemiah returns to Jerusalem and surveys the damage. It must have looked like New York after the September 11 terrorist attacks. Nehemiah assembles the nobles and the officials and simply says, "Let's start building" (Nehemiah 2:11–18). The work of rebuilding is divided up (ch. 3). No one is overwhelmed or discouraged by the enormity of the project because the wall of Jerusalem is rebuilt in small sections.

Often, when a person decides to heal, facing the accumulated damage in his or her life feels overwhelming. Picking up the pieces of a life destroyed by sexual addiction is no small undertaking. If we try to fix everything all at once, we will be discouraged by the enormity of the task. That's why it's important to heed the wisdom of AA's great phrase, "One day at a time." The work of healing happens just that way—one day at a time. A life, a marriage, and a career is also built—and rebuilt— in small parts, one day or one piece at a time.

6. Eliminate Waste and Filth

Nehemiah gives Malkijah and his family the work of rebuilding the Dung Gate (Nehemiah 3:14). Every gate in Jerusalem has a function and through this gate goes the trash, filth, and waste of the entire city. Ever feel like you have a Dung Gate assignment? In truth, this was perhaps the most important gate of all. A city that can't get rid of its waste chokes on its own garbage.

For sex addicts, eliminating filth could mean getting rid of pornography (including Internet accessibility and cable or satellite TV), secret P.O. boxes, bank accounts, affair partners, or even friendships that lead us into trouble. It also means getting rid of the garbage of negative and shameful thoughts, painful memories, anger, resentments, and anxieties.

7. Start Close to Home

Two families build sections of the wall right outside their front door (Nehemiah 3:10).

The people I work with often want to get ahead of themselves. After a recent workshop, a man who had been sexually sober five days e-mailed and said he wanted to write a book about his life so he could help others. I told him to go home, get accountable, serve his wife and family, and e-mail me again after he'd had a year of sobriety. In the beginning especially, accountability doesn't mean going out to save the world. It means staying in to save oneself and one's family.

8. Use Times of Strength to Prepare for Times of Weakness

Later in the story, Nehemiah knows an attack is coming. Israel's enemies are angry that the city they destroyed is being rebuilt. Nehemiah stations twenty-four-hour guards around the wall, especially at its weakest points (Nehemiah 4:9).

In healing from sexual addiction, we know attacks are coming. Satan, our enemy, will tempt us at the weakest places of our defense. Therefore, we must prepare for these attacks. Addicts often say, "When

I am tempted, I will call someone." They fail to recognize that part of the temptation is that they won't want to call anyone. The temptation can reveal they are still invested in the selfish and wounded part of themselves that wants a quick solution.

Preparing for an attack of sexual temptation means planning ahead for times we know we are not strong enough to resist. It could mean we simply ask others to call us regularly. In the first weeks and months of healing, I ask the men I work with to have a regular schedule of men who agree to call them every day, sometimes several times a day.

Preparation also means completely understanding all the elements of one's rituals and putting roadblocks in place. For example, when John travels on business, his ritual is to watch X-rated material in his hotel room, look in the phone book for massage parlors, and then visit one. He puts roadblocks in place by finding hotels that don't offer in-room pornography or he asks the hotel to remove the TV from his room. John leaves phone numbers where he can be reached with his accountability group, and they call him regularly while he is on the road. Andy struggles with Internet pornography, but he needs to use the Internet for his business. He created a roadblock by installing software that tracks his online website visits and sends reports to several of his accountability partners. He knows he is most likely to do this late at night so he asks members of his group to call him then.

Planning ahead like this is not rocket science. People who are willing to be sexually sober do so in times of conviction and strength, knowing there will be future times of weakness.

9. Build Something New in Addition to Defending Against Attacks

Nehemiah has half of his men build and half of his men stand guard and defend the city (Nehemiah 4:16–17). Even the men who carry building materials have a sword in one hand.

In healing from sexual addiction, if all we do is defend, we grow tired and discouraged. We must also build into our lives new behaviors, attitudes, relationships, and spirituality. We are building new lives in Christ, new marriages, and we are always searching for new and deeper ways to connect to God and others. We need to be just as accountable to do the good—rebuilding—as we are accountable to refrain from doing the evil sins we hate.

Alcoholics Anonymous distinguishes it this way. They say a person is "clean" if he or she is avoiding alcohol. They say a person is "sober" if he or she is building a new life. When sex addicts say they are clean and sober, they mean they are avoiding sexual sin *and* they are building new behaviors.

10. Serve Others

Nehemiah says, "Remember the Lord, who is great and awesome, and fight for your brothers, your sons and your daughters, your wives and your homes" (Nehemiah 4:14).

If we are motivated only by selfish fears, we won't get very far. However, if we remain mindful of those we really love, we realize our healing is for them and our motivation is a loving desire to never hurt them again. If we are willing to die to ourselves, we are willing to die for others.

Remember, practicing this kind of accountability can't be done alone or with just one other person. You need a well-organized and well-led support group. This is true for sexual addicts, spouses, and others who seek to lead healthy lives. Over the last several years I have discovered many types of support groups (see Resources on page 228). Like Alcoholics Anonymous for alcoholics, there are Twelve-Step fellowships for sex addicts. In the early days of my recovery, I attended these meetings regularly.

One challenge Christians may have with these groups is that they are not centered in a relationship with Christ and may not emphasize enough the moral and spiritual values we believe in. However, in recent years Christian support groups have been developed that draw on the wisdom of the Twelve Steps. Many of these, such as Faithful and True groups and L.I.F.E. groups, meet in churches. Check to see if these are available in your area. If you can't find a Christian group, consider starting one. The important features of a healthy support group are whether or not it encourages total and rigorous honesty, vulnerability, confession, acts of restitution, accountability (as outlined in this section), and a relationship with Christ.

UNDERSTAND THE PROCESS OF CHANGE

The healing journey is a process of changing old addictive and destructive behaviors into new and healthy ones. It has several stages. I often talk to people who want to be healed in a hurry. They are discouraged at how long the journey takes. But a life that took a lifetime to destroy may take a lifetime to rebuild. Don't be disheartened. Some positive and joyful changes do occur immediately, but enduring and life-transforming change has its ups and downs and is a long journey.

It is helpful to understand the process of change as we embark on the healing journey. Borrowing from the theories of Virginia Satir, a great twentieth-century therapist, let me outline it this way:

Old Behavior	Awareness	Chaos	Practice	New Behavior
Coping	of the need			
Survival	to change			
Familiar				

Figure 8: The Process of Change

Old behavior is sinful and destructive. It is the old status quo. Old behavior is how we have coped and survived since we were children. Like sexual addiction, even though it may be killing us, it is what we know.

Awareness happens when we identify a behavior we need to change. Perhaps someone challenges us or we read about healthy behavior. Or we surrender our lives to Christ and realize we must change our sinful ways. Every sex addict encounters countless times when he or she is aware of the need to change, but old behavior is so familiar and so strong the addict keeps going back to it.

Steve had been looking at pornography and masturbating since he was in middle school. He had also been sexual with several girls in high school. In college he continued this pattern until he met Jean and fell in love. Jean was a Christian and wanted to follow biblical values about sex. Steve went along because he loved her so much. He found himself masturbating more but thought that would stop when he and Jean got married. Steve became a Christian and accepted that he too needed to embrace sexual purity as his goal. Despite this awareness and his love for Jean, he couldn't stop looking at pornography and masturbating.

After getting married and having a normal sexual life with Jean, he was shocked and despondent at his inability to stop.

Chaos occurs when we become willing to change and make real efforts to do so. Since this is new ground, we don't know how to act or what to do. The old behaviors are gone, but we haven't learned new ones yet. Chaos is confusing, frightening, and painful.

Steve finally stopped his sinful sexual behaviors. He was proud of himself for that, but he also became more anxious and depressed. He was confused by this because he thought finding moral "victory" would eliminate his behaviors.

In the next stage of change, we *practice* new awareness, new skills, new relationships, and new spirituality. We keep doing what pastors, counselors, and wiser people tell us to do.

Steve kept going to support group meetings and to therapy. He and Jean also worked hard on new experiences with emotional and spiritual intimacy. It was difficult and there were often setbacks, but Steve held onto his vision of sexual purity.

Ultimately, we practice long enough that new choices become *new behavior*, the new status quo. For sex addicts, sobriety, purity, and fidelity are new behaviors, the new status quo. We also add other new behaviors along the way that impact our faith, our relationships, and all of our actions. Each time we seek to change, we experience a great deal of anxiety and pain. However, as we mature and develop, this anxiety diminishes each time we make healthy changes. This is the journey of healing.

I like to think of the process of change in the context of the epic Old Testament journey that led the Jewish people out of captivity in Egypt and into the Promised Land. Here are several observations about the parallels between the Israelites' journey to freedom and the addict's journey to healing.

Survival Strategies Often Result in Behaviors That Eventually Enslave Us

The last several chapters of Genesis (37–50) tell the story of Joseph and the migration of the Jewish people to Egypt because of a severe famine (Genesis 41:57). They come to Egypt for good reasons—to survive life-threatening hunger. However, after the death of Joseph and the installation of a new Pharaoh, everything changes. The Jewish people have multiplied in their new homeland and the Pharaoh feels threatened. In response, he decides to make them slaves (Exodus 1:6–11).

Just as the Jews came to Egypt to survive a desperate hunger, addicts have deep, unmet emotional and spiritual hungers. We develop coping and survival strategies that seem to feed the hunger for a time, but we eventually find ourselves enslaved by life-threatening, *old behaviors* we can't control or stop.

The Decision to Begin the Healing Journey May Require New Awareness and Many Interventions

God sees the suffering of his people and wants to deliver them. He uses the miracle of a burning bush to create *awareness* of the need in Moses. God calls Moses to leave his comfortable life in Midian and intervene with Pharaoh on behalf of the Jewish people (Exodus 3). When Pharaoh fails to respond to Moses' demands, God sends ten plagues to convince Pharaoh to do so. Eventually, Pharaoh's hard heart is softened and he agrees to release the people from slavery.

Fear Is Often the Greatest Enemy of Meaningful Life Change

God leads the Jewish people back toward the Promised Land and they come to the banks of the Red Sea. Pharaoh regrets his decision to release them and dispatches his armies to bring them back. When the people realize this they are frightened. In the midst of their deliverance, they stand on the banks of their freedom yet long for the safety and familiarity of slavery (Exodus 14:10–14).

This same dynamic is true of life change. Right when we are taking our first steps toward freedom, fear prevents us from going any farther. Suddenly, the pain of the known past feels preferable to the fear of the unknown future. We long to return to what is familiar—even if it is killing us.

The Ability to Face Sadness and
Pain Is Vital to the Healing Journey

Just as the Israelites came face-to-face with what seemed like an insurmountable obstacle in the Red Sea, addicts also face a sea they need to cross. It is the sea of their own tears, what I call the Sea of Sorrows. Most addicts are afraid if they examine their true feelings and life experiences, they will never stop crying. The sadness feels deeper than the sea and overwhelmingly painful.

Mary was a sex addict who had had a number of affairs. One day in therapy she started to sob. Her whole body shook. Suddenly, she stopped and said, "That was really stupid. I just can't let myself be like this." One of the things she learned in childhood was that she needed to be strong and crying was a sign of weakness. Addicts and others must learn that if they allow themselves to dive into their Sea of Sorrows, they won't drown. God is with them and would never let them feel anything they couldn't handle with his help.

The Healing Journey Is
Accomplished One Day at a Time

In the Exodus story, God parts the Red Sea and the Jews cross in safety. When the Egyptians try to cross, God closes the waters and they drown. The Jews have escaped the enemy, but they are now in the desert, the land of *chaos*, and wonder how they will survive. Again the people grumble that life would be better back in Egypt. Despite their ingratitude, God provides manna and quail to feed them, but only enough for one day at a time.

Biblical teaching reminds us again and again that we need to trust God one day at a time. Jesus taught us to pray, "Give us this day our *daily* bread" (see Matthew 6:11; Luke 11:3). In the healing journey, we need to follow this principle as well. If we try to look too far ahead or worry about the future, we diminish our ability to trust God.

We Quench Our Thirst through the Living Water Only God Provides

Next, "The whole Israelite community set out from the Desert of Sin, traveling from place to place as the Lord commanded" (Exodus 17:1). In the desert, the land of chaos, the people are thirsty and have nothing to drink. Again, they complain that slavery in Egypt is preferable to freedom in the desert. Once more, God provides for their needs in miraculous ways. This time he gives them water out of a rock (17:6)!

Addicts come out of sin the same way the Israelites came out of the Desert of Sin—by following God's commands. However, even as we make progress on the healing journey, the temptation persists to quench emotional and spiritual thirsts with old behaviors. Sometimes it may even feel like we will perish without them.

When We Return to True Worship of God, Many Things Can Be Restored

During this time of chaos in the desert, God meets Moses on Mount Sinai to give him stone tablets inscribed with the Ten Commandments (Exodus 20). Moses is away for a long time and the people begin to wonder if both Moses and God have abandoned them. Rather than put their trust in the God who has never failed to provide, the people build and worship false idols made of gold (32:1–6). When Moses returns and sees what the people have done, he throws down the Ten Commandments in anger and smashes them at the foot of the mountain (32:19). God's precious gift to the people is shattered. But Moses reestablishes true worship by destroying the false idols (32:20). He rebukes the people, and then intercedes with God on their behalf. God extends forgiveness and restores to them the Ten Commandments on new stone tablets (34:1).

In the desert chaos of healing from addiction, there may be times when we doubt God's attention to our needs. We may wonder if God has forgotten about us or if he has left us in the middle of our struggles. When fears and anxiety feel overwhelming, it is tempting to break God's commands by placing our trust in false idols, such as old behaviors, and trying to control our own lives. However, the path to genuine healing lies in true worship that centers our trust in God alone. When we do this, God can restore to us many of the precious things our devotion to false idols destroyed.

Relapse Is the Temptation to Go Back to What Is Familiar

Leviticus, the Old Testament book following Exodus, clarifies and expands on many of the laws and commandments God gave to Moses. Leviticus 18 clearly describes God's design for sexuality—we are to be sexual only as husbands and wives.

In Numbers, the next book of the Bible, God commands Moses to pick one man from each of the twelve tribes of Israel to go ahead of the people and scout out the Promised Land (chapter 13). They bring back a good-news/bad-news report. The land does flow with milk and honey, but it also flows with giants. Ten of the twelve scouts are so frightened they shrink back from taking the land God has promised them. When the remaining two, Joshua and Caleb, try to convince the others the land can be conquered with God's help, they are silenced.

On hearing the bad report from the ten scouts, the people weep aloud and once again question why God has brought them out into the desert to die by the sword. They are tired of Moses and want to pick a new leader who will take them back to Egypt (Numbers 14).

In addiction recovery, the first and second years often include obstacles (giants) that seem so formidable we are tempted to give up on the promise of healing. These times are fraught with great potential for relapse. When faced with big challenges, we long to return again to the addiction equivalent of Egypt—the old behaviors that helped us cope in the past.

Taking Risks and Facing Fears Is a Vital Part of the Healing Journey

In our epic story, God's people don't enter the Promised Land for another forty-three years. The generation that came out of Egypt never sets foot in the new homeland. It is only their descendants, led by Joshua, who finally cross the river Jordan. Crossing the river involves great risk. But once the people face their fears and cross over, they are finally able to settle into their new homeland and *practice* a new lifestyle (Joshua 4).

It is facing down the giants of fear and risk that give us the strength and courage we need to enter into new, healthy lifestyles where we finally begin to feel at home.

As Part of the Healing Process, Wiser and More Experienced People May Ask Us to Do Tasks We Don't Readily Understand

Once they have entered the Promised Land, God's people still need to conquer heavily fortified enemy territory. To take the walled city of Jericho, God commands them to march around it once a day for six days, and on the seventh to march around it seven times while blowing trumpets. Can you imagine what the people must have thought about such a command? *Uh, you want us to defeat our vicious enemies with a seven-day parade and some horns?* Yet, when they did so, God honored his promise—the walls came tumbling down and Joshua's army achieved a great victory.

As part of the healing process, there may be times when those who are wiser and more experienced—pastors, counselors, and others—ask us to do things we don't readily understand. This is the way it is in this stage of healing. There are great victories of growth, insight, relationship healing, and deepening faith.

Failing to Keep God's Commands Brings Defeat and Discouragement

Our story is not over, however, and not that easy. One of Joshua's men, Achan, disobeys God's prohibition against keeping any plunder from Jericho. When Joshua sends a small army to take the neighboring city of Ai, the army is routed and thirty-six are killed. At this point, even Joshua is discouraged (Joshua 7:7).

Every victory on the healing journey builds confidence, but victories can also cause overconfidence. Having conquered giants, we may be tempted to reward ourselves in ways that dishonor God. Even if the infractions seem small in light of all we've overcome, they can set us up for defeat when we face the next obstacle. They can also leave us disheartened and discouraged. Even in triumph we need to safeguard our sobriety with obedience to God's commands.

We Must Continue to Trust God More

Ultimately, of course, God's people secure the Promised Land. However, they also continue to question God and rebel against him. Our story is one in which the people are constantly challenged to trust God for their care. God consistently demonstrates that he is trustworthy—from the slavery of Egypt, across the Red Sea, through the chaotic desert, across the river Jordan, and finally into the Promised Land.

There will come a day for healing addicts when sobriety feels solid and stable. However, the struggle isn't over. The healing journey is a constant challenge to trust God more. The process of true change is achieved only as we die to ourselves, relinquish our fears and doubts, depend more on Christ, and surrender to him. As we practice this more and more, God leads us continually away from sinful old behaviors—sexual ones and others—toward new behaviors that are pure, healthy, and life-giving.

At times, we might need to confront those trapped in self-destructive behaviors who are not willing to embark on the healing journey. Addicts who have not yet decided to change are in a state of fear and denial. The next chapter provides guidelines on how and when to conduct an intervention to remove denial and get the addict to seek help.

CHAPTER 9

Confronting
the Sex Addict

If you suspect someone of being a sex addict, you must get the person help before he or she further causes greater destruction to self and others. To ignore this behavior is to become a party to the addict's sin. The process of confronting an addict with his or her behavior is called intervention. This chapter is for those who know or live with a sex addict who is unwilling to seek help.

In Matthew 18:15–17 Jesus outlines a four-step approach for confronting someone who has wronged us. His teaching models Christian conflict resolution, and it also provides an excellent model for conducting an intervention. Jesus describes a four-part process that starts small and builds in intensity depending on the response of the person confronted. First, speak to the person one-to-one: "If the other person listens and confesses it, you have won that person back" (Matthew 18:15 NLT). Second, if you are not successful, go back with one or two others who can confirm what you say. Third, if the person still refuses to listen, take the case to the church. Finally, if the person fails to respond to the discipline of the church, he or she should be put out of the church.

This chapter offers some practical ways of implementing the Matthew 18 principles of conflict resolution and intervention to address sexual addiction.

ONE-TO-ONE INTERVENTION

If you are thinking of confronting a sex addict alone, you first need to take stock of yourself. Consider four questions:

1. Are you able to confront the addict with a spirit of love and gentleness? If you are angry, judgmental, or feeling punitive, ask others to participate in the intervention. The main criterion for any intervention is that it be done in love, not judgment.
2. Are you in a codependent relationship with the addict? If you desperately need a sex addict's approval, you may not have the strength or the objectivity to confront the addict on your own.
3. Is your own conscience clear in this area? Most sex addicts can tell you about people who were angry with them about their sexual behaviors yet had committed the same behaviors themselves.
4. Will you be able to follow through on the intervention? Personal intervention includes establishing ultimatums and following through on them. Never attempt this kind of intervention if you are not strong enough to do what you say you're going to do.

If you feel prepared to proceed with the intervention, tell someone else about your plan. Telling someone provides accountability and gives you the strength and courage to follow through. It also helps to talk through your motivations and assure you are taking action out of love, not judgment.

The goal of an intervention is to force the addict to seek help. Before initiating a conversation with the addict, find out where help is available and how to get it. Collect a list of phone numbers for counselors, treatment centers, and Twelve-Step fellowships. As part of the intervention, be prepared to drive the person to a counselor, or perhaps even offer to help pay for therapeutic help.

Once you have taken stock of yourself, assessed your motives, and gathered information about treatment resources, courageously confront the person in a one-to-one conversation. Address only the behaviors you know about. You might begin by saying, "I care about you, but I am concerned about some of your behaviors. By those I mean ... [list the facts of the sexual acting out]."

If applicable, share your own weaknesses and experience of getting help. For example, "I know what it's like to do these things. These are some of the addictive behaviors I have done ... [describe them]. I was out of control and I was afraid if people knew what I was doing, they would hate me. Finally, I found help ... [describe your process of getting help]." If you can't relate personally to the sexual or addictive behaviors, you might describe someone you know about [without mentioning names] who had similar problems and got help.

Try to empathize with the sex addict: "It must be really lonely. You must be tired and frightened," or "You may be angry with me for bringing this up." Avoid diagnosing the problem. Don't say, "You must come from a really screwed-up family." Also avoid judgmental comments: "How could you do such things? Didn't you know any better?"

Carefully distinguish the impact the sex addict's behavior has on you from the impact it has on others. "When you did ... [list a behavior], it really hurt me and I got angry," or "That really embarrassed me or caused me harm ... [describe the exact nature of the harm]." Do not list harms to others, at least not at this time. This only serves to make the sex addict defensive. If a sex addict does become defensive, you might say, "I'm not trying to judge you, and right now I don't need you to defend your behaviors. I need you to listen to what I'm saying. I just want you to know how your behaviors have affected me."

Next state how you would like the sex addict's behavior to change in relationship to you. For example, "Please do not tell sexual jokes around me anymore." If you're a spouse, this might include statements like, "Please do not ask me for sex. Please don't touch me in that way. Please don't ask me for ... [describe certain sexual behaviors]. I expect you to be sexually faithful to me."

Then describe the consequences to the sex addict if he or she is not able to observe the stated boundaries. "If you do these things again, I will ... [describe the exact nature of what you will do]." For a spouse, this might be, "If you continue these sexual behaviors, I won't be able to live under the same roof with you. I can't stand to see you destroying yourself, our marriage, and our family." An employer might state obvious vocational consequences. A pastor could state consequences in terms of church membership.

Restate your love and concern for the addict. "I care for you. I value our relationship and want to see it continue. I hope and pray you get help." State your faith in a personal God who loves and cares for the sex addict, and affirm your belief in Scriptures that underline God's love and acceptance for the repentant sinner.

A sex addict might be very defensive about religion. Never argue or get defensive in return. To do so is the quickest way to end the conversation. Instead, say something like, "It must be really hard to have prayed and not get the answer you want. I sometimes believe God works in quiet, less dramatic ways than we might expect. Sometimes I don't understand how God works. All I know right now is that I'm willing to help you . . . [list the ways you are willing to help]."

The worst-case scenario is that the sex addict won't listen to you, won't accept help, or will become angry. If this happens, it can be very discouraging. Find support from those who have supported you in the past. You may need to talk to your pastor or a therapist about how much this has disappointed you and what you should do next. Remember that the addict's anger or defensiveness has nothing to do with what you have done, how you have done it, or with you as a person. Sexual addiction is a powerful disease. A sex addict's reaction is a symptom of how tightly the disease still controls him or her.

GROUP INTERVENTION

Sex addicts who don't respond to one-to-one intervention require group intervention. As Jesus instructs, take one or two others to support you and to provide more evidence. Sex addicts who deny they have a problem need to be confronted with evidence—undeniable statements that prove they have a problem. Sex addicts are very skilled at deceiving others. They may easily talk their way out of accusations from one person, but denial and deception is much more difficult when two or three people all affirm seeing the sinful behavior.

I once worked at a hospital that specialized in treating addicted professionals such as doctors, lawyers, and pastors. These patients almost always came to us after being confronted in a group setting. One of my colleagues, Dr. Richard Irons, used to say that individually confronting these addicts was like playing one-on-one basketball against former NBA superstar Michael Jordan—no one person could win. However, he pointed out that when we take a team of people, even if none of them are of NBA caliber, the team almost always gets the job done.

Before participating in an intervention, it is important to understand the roles of the group moderator and group participants, the logistics of group process, and some unique family dynamics.

Group Moderator

Group interventions need a facilitator or moderator. This can be a counselor or pastor experienced in the art of group intervention. Some professionals specialize in interventions. If you have difficulty finding a referral for a moderator, contact one of the treatment programs listed on pages 228–33 in the Resources section. The role of the moderator is extremely important. His or her goal is to orchestrate the intervention in the way most likely to result in the sex addict agreeing to get help.

Group Participants

Group interventions can include a wide range of participants. The classic alcoholic intervention includes family members, friends, employers, church members, and any other concerned people who have knowledge of the facts and have been impacted by the addict's behavior. The moderator assesses if any person intending to participate lacks the maturity or emotional objectivity to effectively do so. For example, family members just learning about the severity of the sex addict's behaviors may be so caught up in their own hurt and anger it would be difficult for them to participate without losing control emotionally. Such reactions would only cause the sex addict to be defensive or distracted from the primary objective of the intervention.

Group Process

Often a moderator gathers the group together before the intervention. In this meeting the moderator hears the facts, gathers information about each person's boundaries, fully accounts for consequences that might take place if the addict is not willing to get help, and provides a complete list of treatment resources as well as a list of people willing to assist the addict in getting that help. The moderator might also help participants rehearse what to say, and how and when to say it.

How do you get an addict to a group intervention? It is almost always done by surprise. If addicts have enough time to anticipate what is coming, they probably won't come. The process is not unlike what some people go through to throw a surprise birthday party. Some excuse is made to get the person to a place where others are waiting for them. That is the way of intervention.

The moderator leads the entire meeting, calling on people to speak at appropriate times. The moderator might begin by saying, "We are here because we love you and because we are very concerned about you. We are not here to judge you, but we do need to talk with you about certain behaviors that deeply concern us." The group intervention then follows the same process as the one-to-one intervention described above. Each participant expresses care and concern, provides evidence, articulates the impact the sexual behaviors have had on them personally, defines boundaries, establishes consequences, and offers help.

If the sex addict resists all these steps, those involved must not associate with that person. A spouse should take steps to separate from the addict, friends should refuse to socialize with the addict, and the church should bar the addict from participating in the Lord's Supper. Shunning a person is intensely painful for everyone, but it is the most caring thing to do, and the most honest. The sexual behaviors involved, whatever they are, are intolerable and must stop. Only by facing the consequences of their behavior will some addicts be shaken into acknowledgment of their problem.

All participants must discipline themselves to enforce the consequences stipulated in the intervention. If sex addicts get away with their behavior, they will believe they have manipulated the system again and can repeat the behaviors without suffering consequences.

Family Dynamics

Occasionally, family members deny the addict's behavior as vehemently as the sex addicts themselves. As I have said, the family—especially the spouse—is often the last to accept the reality of inappropriate sexual behaviors. However, even if the sex addict has been very good at deceiving them, at some gut level they know what is going on, and discovering the truth will make sense to them. In these cases, group interventions involve those who accept the truth and are willing to take action. Family members who have not accepted the problem should not be present at the intervention. They should, however, be kept informed about the plan of action.

Sometimes family members may be as sick as the sex addict. If those planning an intervention are not family members themselves, planners need to be aware they are dealing with the family as well as the addict. Be prepared to provide care for family members before and after an intervention and also have resource lists available to help meet their needs.

Interventions are highly emotional. There may be anger, denial, delusions, and high drama. Sex addicts may deny their behavior entirely, or play the role of victim. Sometimes a sex addict uses religious forms of denial to avoid getting help. I witnessed a recent intervention in which a group of church leaders and their pastor conducted an intervention with a member who'd had a number of affairs with women in the church. The man became intensely emotional, crying and asking for God's forgiveness. His behavior, however, didn't change. This same group intervened again. Once more, the man cried for forgiveness. However, this time the group asked him to leave the church until he could demonstrate ongoing sexual sobriety. The man became furious and accused the group of not practicing God's love and forgiveness. In a short time, he managed to create divisions in the church—all in the name of God's love and forgiveness.

Those who intervene have a very difficult task. Participating in an intervention challenges all of one's emotional vulnerabilities. If you are part of an intervention team, I strongly encourage you to find support for yourself in this process. Even if you start with a one-to-one intervention, it's best to first have the guidance and support of a pastor or therapist. Make sure that after an intervention you schedule time with members of your support system to debrief the experience. You will need their affirmation and assurance that you did the right thing.

Even though I have been involved in many interventions, they still take a toll on me. I never go into these situations without earnestly praying first. It calms me down and enables me to trust God for guidance. Recently, I was involved in an intervention on a pastor. He became very emotional and dramatic and started quoting Scripture and preaching about forgiveness. He was loud and obnoxious. He told all of us we were there to do "the devil's work." Afterward, I knew I needed to connect with professional friends who could remind me of the truth we knew about this man and that we had initiated the intervention in love.

When an intervention goes well and the addict agrees to seek treatment, the next step is finding that treatment. Chapter 10 describes what to look for when seeking effective treatment resources.

CHAPTER 10

TREATMENT ISSUES
IN SEXUAL ADDICTION

Once an addict has agreed to get treatment for sexual addiction, the first step is to find someone who can assess the addict and make a formal diagnosis of sexual addiction. A growing number of Christian counselors are trained to do this. They ask for a history of behaviors and feelings and give their opinion about an appropriate course of treatment. Written diagnostic tests are also available. The oldest and the most widely validated instruments are the Sexual Addiction Screening Test (SAST) and the Sexual Addiction Inventory (SAI). The SAST is very short and the SAI is very long.[1] Even though one of these tests is available online, be careful of self-diagnosis. Reading books or taking online tests is a good way to raise awareness, but ultimately a professional opinion is essential.

Once a formal diagnosis of sexual addiction is made, five basic components of treatment based on the sexual addiction cycle are vital to recovery (see figure 9). These include stopping sexual behaviors, stopping rituals, stopping fantasy, healing despair, and healing shame.

An effective treatment plan includes elements of all five components. Each component should be addressed at some level from the beginning, but stopping sexual behaviors is the first priority. Working on one component effects work on another. Effective treatment is cyclical, and experiencing success in one area promotes results in all com-

---

Healing Shame

- Confession of sin and repentance
- Practicing spiritual disciplines
- Healing trauma
- Belonging to an affirming church and social community

Stopping Fantasy

- Understand the three objectives of fantasy
- Discover what the fantasies symbolize and what needs of the wounded self they represent
- Make healthy choices to get needs met

Healing Despair

- Finding God
- Asking for forgiveness
- Admitting being out of control
- Affirmations from others
- Hearing the stories of others

Stopping Rituals

- Identify ritual behaviors
- Establish roadblocks
- Develop healthy emotional, physical, and spiritual rituals

Stopping Sexual Behaviors

- Abstinence contract
- Accountability plan
- Counseling
- Medical help
- Outpatient and intensive programs
- Inpatient treatment

Figure 9: The Five Components of Treatment

ponents of the cycle. Finding sobriety, for example, reduces despair and shame.

This chapter is divided into two parts. The first part describes in priority order the five components of treatment. The second part describes additional treatment issues that impact all five components in some way.

The healing process is a lot of work. It can feel very daunting and discouraging—and it is. But the work is worth it. Over the years I, and many other therapists, have seen a direct correlation between how much work people invest in treatment and how permanent and stable their sobriety is. The AA tradition says we must "be willing to go to any length to recover," and also, "half-measures avail us nothing." This is not meant to be a pep talk so much as an encouragement—all the work is infinitely worthwhile for the healing and sobriety it brings.

THE FIVE COMPONENTS OF TREATMENT

Stopping Sexual Behaviors

The first step is stopping sexual behaviors. This includes the three building-block behaviors—fantasy, masturbation, use of pornography—and any other behaviors addicts may have engaged in. Just as alcoholics need to stop drinking before they can be treated, sex addicts need to stop acting out before they can embark on the healing journey.

Tools and resources available to help addicts stop sexual behaviors include an abstinence contract, counseling, medical help, outpatient and intensive programs, and inpatient treatment.

Abstinence Contract

It is vitally important for sex addicts to stop all sexual behaviors for at least ninety days. They should agree to an abstinence or celibacy contract, which states they will not be sexual with themselves (through masturbation) or anyone else, including a spouse. This contract achieves two basic purposes—one physiological and one intellectual. First, prolonged lack of sexual activity reverses the level of neuro-chemical tolerance addicts have built into their brains. Addicts may experience symptoms of detoxification not unlike an alcoholic, though not as severe. Most people really struggle with this contract somewhere between the seventh to fourteenth day depending on their past levels of sexual activity. After that, abstinence gets easier over time. Second, abstinence reverses the sex addict's core belief that "Sex is my most important need." Instead, the sex addict discovers, "Sex is *not* my most important need." This is why ninety days (though somewhat arbitrary) is symbolically important.

Married sex addicts commit to this contract with the mutual consent of their spouse. In 1 Corinthians 7:5 Paul writes, "Do not deprive each other [sexually] except by mutual consent and for a time, so that you may devote yourselves to prayer." Paul's teaching instructs us to replace sexuality, for a time, with prayer. I believe advocating prayer is Paul's way of saying that couples need to develop a deeper spiritual life together. In addition to prayer there may be other spiritual disciplines a couple chooses to do, such as Bible study, reading a book of meditations, or attending worship together.

Spouses often welcome the abstinence contract because the addict has been continually initiating for years. Some are afraid of it because they believe if they are not sexual with the addict, it will discourage him or her from getting sober. Others resent the contract because they worry what they will do without sex. Sometimes it is best to negotiate the abstinence contract with a pastor or counselor to avoid misunderstandings about the nature and purpose of the contract. A spouse should be aware that the frequency of sex is *never* a factor in determining if a sex addict stays sober.

Abstinence can't continue forever if the sex addict is married. In this regard, recovering from sexual addiction is not like recovering from alcoholism. Alcoholics can abstain from alcohol for the rest of their lives, but sex addicts do not usually abstain from sex. Recovering from sexual addiction is more analogous to recovering from food addiction. Food addicts can't stop eating forever, but they can learn to eat to nourish themselves when their bodies are hungry. Married sex addicts learn that sex with a spouse is appropriate and beautiful when, instead of being a way to avoid intimacy or escape negative feelings, it expresses the intimacy of the marriage.

Counseling

Some sex addicts achieve sobriety simply by going to support groups. However, most sex addicts also need counseling. The deep emotional and spiritual issues associated with sexual addiction require the care and guidance of a trained professional. I am a strong believer in finding a Christian counselor who really knows the field of sexual addiction. A counselor who is well versed in biblical, spiritual, deep emotional, and behavioral counseling is also very important.

There are various levels of counselors. Some pastors are well trained, though many are not. Pastors may have advanced degrees, such as a master of divinity or a doctor of ministry. Some counselors have doctoral degrees, such as a Ph.D., and others have only a masters degree. Most qualified counselors are licensed by their state or are certified by a professional counseling organization. In some cases lay counselors are able to help at initial levels.[2]

Medical Help

Medical evaluations are strongly advised. Given the probable presence of other mental health issues, such as depression, anxiety, and attentional disorders, it is important that sex addicts have thorough medical evaluations. Though some family practice physicians are capable of this kind of evaluation, it is usually far better to consult a psychiatrist competent in working with addiction. A growing number of psychiatric clinics use brain scan imaging, such as SPEC scans or Functional MRIs, as part of their evaluations. In some very difficult cases, it may be necessary to find one of those clinics.

Outpatient and Intensive Programs

If support meetings, counseling, and medical evaluation are not enough to stop sexual behaviors, the next step is an outpatient or intensive treatment program, similar to such programs for alcoholism. These programs provide three to four hours of treatment per day, three to five days a week. The addict is usually allowed to live at home or in a nearby hotel. Outpatient and intensive programs provide therapy, group support, and education. In many programs, spouses and families are involved as well.

Over the last ten years, a number of five-day workshops have been developed for sex addicts, their spouses, and for couples.[3] These workshops provide teaching and small group experiences. Addicts, spouses, and couples explore the nature of their addictions, co-addictions, or relationship issues. They also explore early life wounds and receive practical guidance about healing. These workshops often "jump-start" an addict six to twelve months ahead on the healing journey.

Inpatient Treatment

In some cases, aggressive inpatient treatment is needed. This means a residential, hospital-based unit in which the addict stays in treatment full time. Hospital programs are vital for sex addicts experiencing severe depression or suicidal thoughts. For their own safety, around-the-clock care is essential. Inpatient programs are usually supervised by medical doctors and provide twenty-four-hour nursing care. Competent therapists, counselors, or psychiatrists provide counseling.

These programs vary in length from two to five weeks. One of these weeks may include family members who accept the addict's invitation to attend. This week is part of the total treatment plan and is called "family week."

Inpatient programs are expensive and often cost-prohibitive. In the last ten years, these programs have become increasingly less available due to diminished insurance coverage. A person typically has to be diagnosed with major depression to get insurance to cover the cost for just a few days. Those who really need or want inpatient treatment typically have to pay for it themselves.

Each of these treatment levels—from abstinence contracts to inpatient treatment—represents increasingly tighter control over the sex addict's environment and greater levels of support and supervision. Ultimately, even in inpatient programs, sex addicts must learn to monitor themselves.

Stopping Rituals

Stopping rituals is key to stopping sexual acting out. Rituals are all the thoughts and actions that lead to sexual acting out. If alcoholics allow themselves to go into a bar, they will probably take a drink. Drinking is acting out. Going to the bar is the ritual. The same is true for sex addicts. If they allow themselves to engage in their rituals, acting out will follow.

Identify Ritual Behaviors

In the early days of recovery, sex addicts usually have no idea that rituals precede their sexual behaviors. Most support groups, treatment programs, and workshops for addicts are designed to help them understand and identify their rituals. Addicts often learn about themselves by hearing about the behavior and rituals of others. Every addict's rituals are unique but the principle is the same—rituals precede acting out.

Rituals can be short or long in duration. Shorter rituals are easiest to identify and understand, and longer rituals are more difficult. Masturbation and pornography rituals are typically brief and daily in nature. Some sex addicts pursue a short ritual after being triggered by a stimulus on TV or the Internet. They get into their cars, get money at an instant-teller machine, and go to a massage parlor. Other sex addicts pursue longer rituals by recruiting potential partners, developing a friendship over weeks, months, or even years, and eventually acting out sexually with them.

Establish Roadblocks

Once addicts identify their rituals, they need to establish roadblocks to prevent the rituals from taking place. For example, if the ritual involves viewing Internet pornography and then masturbating, establishing a roadblock could mean completely discontinuing Internet use or installing a filter and a monitoring service. If the addict's ritual is a series of lunches alone with potential affair partners, such lunches cannot be allowed. These two examples are relatively obvious. Sex addicts have to evaluate what roadblocks to establish for themselves based on identifying their rituals.

For pastors, the whole pastoral role may be part of the ritual. They may not be aware of this, but the power, authority, and spirituality they represent attracts others to them. The way they teach, preach, counsel, and care for others may all be part of the rituals sexually addicted pastors must give up, at least for a time.

The actions that must be taken to stop rituals are called healthy boundaries. Sex addicts in recovery must identify what healthy boundaries are for them. In the early days, boundaries may need to be stricter than in later years, but the guiding principle is, "I must go to any length to recover." Support groups, sponsors, counselors, and treatment providers are skilled in educating sex addicts about their rituals. Addicts typically make lists of their rituals and the healthy boundaries they must maintain to prevent the rituals from happening. Maintaining these boundaries is the key to stopping rituals.

Develop Healthy Emotional, Physical, and Spiritual Disciplines and Rituals

Positive discipline establishes new, positive rituals for the sex addict. If sex addicts bring the same energy to new rituals that they devoted to the old ones, they will be extremely successful. The book of Hebrews says, "My child, don't ignore it when the Lord disciplines you, and don't be discouraged when he corrects you" (Hebrews 12:5). Discipline has both the negative aspect of punishment and the positive aspect of learning healthy behaviors. Healthy discipline maintains healthy boundaries that can be emotional, physical, sexual, and certainly spiritual in nature.

Healthy emotional boundaries result in addicts feeling better about themselves. They should beware, however, of all those people or books that tell them to start liking themselves. For sex addicts who are abuse victims, it is never that easy.

The key is discipline, starting with what the recovery community calls "self-talk," messages that addicts daily remind themselves. Sex addicts might make a list of the good things in their life. At first, they might not believe these affirmations. Belief will come after the discipline of practice. One of the old AA slogans says, "Fake it till you make it." For addicts, as for all of us, this means that we decide to think or act in healthy ways even if we don't feel like it. After a time of doing so, the thoughts or actions come more naturally. For example, an addict can decide to forgive someone who has harmed them even though he doesn't feel like it. He acts accordingly. Eventually he may start feeling the spirit of forgiveness. Feeling forgiving will help avoid the feeling of resentment. Anger and resentment lead to thought rituals such as "I deserve to get my needs met," and this leads to acting out.

Sex addicts should make a point of associating with people who affirm them. They should make a list of people who help them feel good about themselves, and a second list of people to avoid—those who make them feel ashamed. They need to tell themselves, "I deserve to be with loving and affirming people. I can avoid people, including family members, who only tell me shaming messages."

Physical discipline is easier to understand than emotional discipline. Sex addicts may not have taken care of themselves for years. They must learn, for example, to eat nutritious foods, get enough sleep, exercise regularly, or stop smoking. It is always amazing to find out how much better they will feel emotionally and spiritually if they do some of these things. Anything done to nourish oneself in positive physical ways is also having a healthy physical relationship with oneself. Think of simple things like buying nice sheets for your bed, taking a bubble bath, exercising regularly, or getting a manicure. A healthy sexual relationship in a marriage depends on each partner respecting and nurturing his or her own body.

It is vitally important that sex addicts also incorporate spiritual disciplines into their recovery process. Spiritual disciplines include prayer, Bible study, meditation, church, spiritual direction, and retreats. Doing these disciplines may be hard because of shame. Addicts may not feel worthy of a relationship with God. In the early days of recovery, guides and mentors will be necessary to gently help them acquire the discipline necessary to overcome shame. Often, in my experience, support groups function like church would. They become the healthy community that addicts need to experience grace.

Stopping the sexual behaviors and rituals are the most important early priorities to establish sobriety. Next, an addict must examine the fantasies that drive them.

Stopping Fantasy

Stopping fantasy is perhaps one of the hardest aspects of recovery. Addicts can simply think about their behaviors for stimulation—and a sex addict has countless memories and fantasies to draw on. Sights, sounds, words, and people can instantly trigger a fantasy. Trying to stop is extremely frustrating because these images can't be erased.

Traditional approaches to stopping fantasy include encouraging the addict to simply stop, think of something else, or to do something negative when fantasies occur so they associate pain or punishment with fantasy. None of these approaches is very effective. Addicts have played too many mind games and have too many stimuli locked away in their memories to simply stop the fantasy or to think of something else. The problem with associating pain with fantasy is that sex remains or becomes a completely negative experience. If addicts condition themselves to associate sex with pain, at what point do they experience healthy and positive sexuality? I do not recommend these strategies.

Fantasies don't develop randomly or without reason, they have a purpose. In order to stop them, we must first understand their purpose.

Fantasy Has Three Objectives

Fantasy is a symptom of the emotional and spiritual condition of sex addicts. When they are lonely, tired, angry, sad, anxious, or afraid, their fantasies take over their thinking. Fantasies accomplish three objectives: distracting addicts from painful emotions, meeting addicts' otherwise unmet desires and needs, and recasting addicts' experiences of past abuse.

First, fantasizing distracts addicts from painful feelings. Even fantasizing about sex can create all the neurochemistry of the sexual response. Exciting, new, and perhaps dangerous fantasies elevate mood. Romantic and connecting fantasies calm mood. Fantasies, therefore, have the capability to either raise or lower mood.

The second objective of fantasies is to fill deep desires addicts feel they can't fill any other way. When addicts feel they haven't been heard, affirmed, blessed, loved, nurtured, and touched in healthy ways, fantasies create scenarios in which all these needs are met. There can be many types of fantasies. Most of us have some kind or another. We might dream of athletic, monetary, role, status, or power fantasies. Any of these fantasies might allow us to imagine we are really special people deserving of love and attention. Sexual fantasies are like that. In them, the addict is always heard, touched, included, affirmed and praised, and loved. Although it is a false solution, a false idol, it is the way the addict has coped for years.

The third objective of sexual fantasies is that they enable the addict to replay past sexual abuse experiences (perhaps in symbolic ways), but with two potential differences: either there is a different outcome to the activity, or the addict gets to be the initiator rather than the victim.

Fantasies are almost always symbolic of deep wounds and unmet needs. The most effective way to stop fantasies is not to ignore them but to understand what they mean, to identify the family-of-origin and abuse issues they represent, and to then make healthy choices to get needs met.

Discover What the Fantasies Symbolize and What Needs of the Wounded Self They Represent

Every sexual fantasy has symbolic meaning. To stop fantasies, it is important to first understand what they represent. Sometimes the personality or appearance of a person(s) who shows up in a fantasy represents the person who most profoundly abandoned the addict. In the fantasy, however, the person is completely loving in ways the addict needs to be loved. The type of sexual activity is also highly symbolic. It may re-create exciting early sexual experiences, symbolize total acceptance, or represent consuming the essence of the sexual partner.

Talking about stopping sexual behaviors, rituals, and fantasies is extremely threatening to sex addicts, for these behaviors have helped them survive. Perhaps the addict was abandoned as a three-year-old. Frightened and alone, she turned to behaviors that calmed her and allowed her to escape, at least in her mind. Would she not cling to that behavior? Only in later life does she learn these behaviors will also kill her. Somehow, this doesn't make sense. How could something so helpful be so deadly? This confusion is a barrier to giving up addictive behavior.

Sex addicts are adults who know their behavior is dangerous. Yet inside them is a child who knows giving up that behavior will cause great pain. Addicts' lives are a tug-of-war between the adult and the child. Before addicts can find healing and become fully adult, they must confront the fears of the child within. I discuss this kind of inner healing below in "Healing Abuse."

Make Healthy Choices to Get Needs Met

In recovery, addicts must be taught they have choices about dealing with painful feelings. When they are tired and lonely and beginning to fantasize, they can ask themselves, "What does this fantasy mean? What am I feeling? Am I sad, lonely, afraid, or what?" They can call someone to talk to. They can go to a meeting. The key is learning to tell someone what the feelings are and getting the support they need.

Healing Despair

Sex addicts experience deep emotional and spiritual despair. They believe there is no hope, that life will never get better, and that, if there is a God, he doesn't care. Many despairing addicts consider suicide.

Although despair seems to be a negative emotion, it can lead to positive change. Despair forces addicts to face the facts—that their efforts are never effective, they need other people, and they need God. When this happens, feelings of despair can actually lead to surrender to God. If you love and care for an addict, resist the temptation to rush in and alleviate the addict's despair with quick or simplistic solutions. God may be at work in the despair to bring about lasting change in the addict's life.

As sex addicts begin to recover from addictive behavior, they slowly recover from despair as well. When in despair, hearing testimonies of other recovering addicts is especially encouraging. Discovering that people can change and learning that life does get better provides hope and motivation to stay on the healing path. Addicts gain self-confidence as they learn to control sexual behavior, rituals, and fantasies. They grow stronger by admitting their addiction and testifying to their recovery. This gradual process of encouragement and self-affirmation diminishes feelings of despair and also begins to heal the addict's sense of shame.

Healing Shame

Like despair, shame is not all bad. Shame points us to our own unworthiness and our need for God. Abuse victims, however, often assume an identity of shame and feel completely worthless.

To deal with unhealthy shame, sex addicts must delve into any trauma and wounds they have experienced. I strongly recommend group therapy in addition to individual counseling because many addicts learn about their own abuse by watching other addicts deal with theirs. They may have repressed memories of abuse because they are so painful. Observing others accept and deal with abuse helps addicts feel safe enough to let their own memories return to consciousness.

Painful memories come back as the addict is ready to deal with them. I believe God is in control of this process and does not give addicts more to cope with than they are prepared to handle. It is always wise for addicts to pray that God through the power of the Holy Spirit will show them what they need to heal from in God's own perfect timing.

It may take years for a sex addict to recall and deal with memories of abuse. If the abuse is more severe, it will take longer. It is not uncommon for some memories of abuse to surface right away and for others to come later. One female addict, for example, recalled childhood incest with her father only after eighteen months of counseling. Because she was in a community where she felt safe, her mind allowed her to remember this extremely significant abuse.

Sex addicts may be discouraged that this process takes so long and is so painful. However, the intensity of the experiences diminishes over time and periods of joy and peace increase. As they recover from their addiction, tell others what they have done, learn to share who they really are, and make amends, addicts find healing from their sense of shame. After they have been angry about wounds, they learn to find peace in forgiving those who harmed them, just as they have asked forgiveness from those they have harmed.

Only God can truly heal the sense of shame. Christ died not only to take away our sins, but also to vanquish our shame. Through him we will find freedom from shame, despair, and addiction. The ultimate way to heal from shame and wounds is to find meaning in them.

Every time I share my pain with others and they are able to share their pain with me, it connects us to each other. Whenever this happens, my pain feels lighter. My shame and wounds are also my opportunity to participate in the pain that all people experience. And this is what Christ did—he came to earth and shared our pain. Jesus knew doubt, anxiety, betrayal, pain, and abandonment. As I understand that God, in Christ, shares in my pain, it becomes lighter and easier to bear.[4] Addicts on the ultimate healing journey do not ask that the pain of the past be taken away. It is their chance to experience true fellowship with Christ and with others.

ADDITIONAL TREATMENT ISSUES IN THE HEALING PROCESS

Sexual addiction is a lifelong disease. The treatment strategies presented in the first half of this chapter describe the healing that needs to take place in the first several years of recovery. This is the most intense period of healing. Sex addicts will always need to go to meetings, get counseling, have a sponsor, and maintain spiritual disciplines. When they do these things, they continue to grow in all areas of their lives.

The following are additional issues that need to be dealt with in the recovery process: understanding abuse, healing relationships, codependency, slips and relapse, and deepening spirituality. Hard work on these issues contributes to the overall effectiveness of the five components of treatment described above.

Healing Abuse

Sex addicts need to deal with the abuse they suffered in the past. Over the years, I have found it helpful to think of this healing in six stages.

1. Understand the Abuse and Accept That It Happened

Addicts may or may not be able to fully remember the abuse they experienced, depending on how young they were at the time and how violent it was. Therapy provides a safe environment in which sex addicts may remember what needs to be remembered. In groups, others dealing with their abuse may help addicts remember what happened to them. At other times, education about abuse is enough to trigger memories.

Because of shame, sex addicts do not want to accept their abuse, even the most obvious and violent kinds. A part of them believes they are responsible for the abuse and even deserved it. They need direct, assertive, and continuing support to counteract such misguided beliefs.

2. Accept the Abuse and Express Anger

The addict's high pain threshold causes them to minimize the effects of abuse. They want to forgive and forget, move on, and think only about the future. However, they need to be gently reminded that strength comes not by denying their feelings, but by embracing them. Anger is one of the most difficult emotions to learn to express in healthy ways. When anger is not dealt with, however, it can express itself in a variety of unhealthy ways.

3. Go Through the Process of Grieving

Recovering sex addicts must learn to grieve. They must mourn the fact that the love they needed as a child can never be replaced. The pain of this realization can be overwhelming, and addicts need support to help them experience and understand these feelings.

4. Confront the Abuser

There is some controversy about whether or not to confront abusers. Some say that the act of confrontation is symbolic of accepting the abuse as powerful and of retaking control over it. When addicts confront abuse they establish that the abuser no longer has power to hurt them. On the negative side, such confrontation can be unnecessarily hurtful, particularly if the abuser doesn't have the resources, awareness, or emotional and spiritual health to deal positively with the hurt in healing ways. This can only lead to distance and prevent the possibility of future reconciliation.

I believe confronting the abuse can happen without direct confrontations of the abusers. There are other forms of dealing with the abuse that don't require direct confrontation. Addicts can express emotions in therapy or write but not mail letters to the abuser. Addicts can also role-play confrontation with other group therapy participants. These approaches can be emotionally healing without doing more damage. Whenever addicts, as victims, engage in such indirect expressions of their feelings, they must always be reminded of the truth about their abuse—that it was not their fault, they didn't deserve for it to happen, and God loves them as they are.

An abuser may need to be confronted if the abuse is ongoing or if the potential for it to continue is great. Charlie, for example, was sexually abused by his father when he was a small boy. In therapy he had worked through this very well and didn't feel the direct need to confront his dad about it. However, confrontation become necessary when Charlie began to suspect his dad might be abusing one of his sons. Direct confrontation should be done in the presence of a mediator, such as a therapist or a pastor. The mediator's job is to assure the confrontation process is constructive. Even though the addict expresses anger, he can do so in nonjudgmental ways by stating he is doing this to heal himself and to prevent the abuser from hurting others. The addict may even say that he is confronting the abuser in order to heal or reconcile their relationship.

Legal authorities may need to be involved if the victim is still a minor or was a vulnerable adult at the time of the abuse. In most states, it is mandatory to report such abuse. A vulnerable adult is a person who does not have the capacity to say no because of emotional limitations, such as mental retardation, or is under the emotional and spiritual influence of the abuser. An adult parishioner, for example, is considered to be under the emotional and spiritual influence of a pastor or priest. Doctors, lawyers, and teachers also fall into the category of those who have such authority. Many female addicts, for example, had sex with a pastor, doctor, teacher, or lawyer. Even though it seemed consensual, the law considers it abuse of power.

Legal authorities also need to be notified if there is a possibility the abuser is still abusing vulnerable children or adults. Jay is a sex addict who can't stop masturbating, viewing pornography, and visiting prostitutes. A priest abused him when he was fifteen. Even though Jay is now an adult, he must report the priest because there is the possibility he is still abusing boys. This can be difficult to do emotionally, but when the motivation is to protect others, it should be done.

5. Learn to Forgive

Addicts heal abuse by coming to a spirit of forgiveness. While addicts should not be too quick to forgive and should fully experience their grief and anger, they eventually need to move through the stages of healing them. Forgiveness becomes possible after anger and confrontation. It may help addicts decide to forgive when they realize their abusers may also have been abused. One addict said, "It is easy to see why my father did what he did to me. I know my grandfather! My dad did to me what was done to him." Earlier, I described that an addict may choose to forgive even though he doesn't feel like it. Acting like a forgiving person can be an important part of the healing strategy.

6. Find Meaning in the Pain

Ultimately, healing abuse is a matter of finding meaning in the pain. This is spiritual transformation. The apostle James writes that we should consider it joy to experience various pains (or trials) because such tests of our faith produces stronger faith (James 1:2–3).

In the healing journey, addicts gradually begin to stop fighting against the pain of their wounds. They stop wishing the abuse had never happened and that they had had different families or life circumstances. They begin to see that their pain, unique as it is to them, is also their opportunity to connect to the pain of others. Connecting in this way with others, including one's spouse, is the deepest, most intimate connection there is. It is why so many of us go to meetings and support groups where we find others who have experienced similar pain. In fellowship we find that we connect in our weaknesses and not our strengths. Knowing this prepares us for healthy relationships.

Healing Relationships

Chapter 11 specifically addresses healing for couples. However, sex addicts, must heal all significant relationships. This takes time but healing starts in the first months and years of recovery.

Key to the process is honesty. For years sex addicts have been dishonest and deceptive with others. To heal relationships, they must be honest and no longer lie about their behavior. Healthy relationships depend on honesty. Addicts, however, don't need to go out and shout the truth to the whole world. They need to pick people who are safe and healthy enough to receive the addict's vulnerability.

Addicts must take responsibility for their problems and stop blaming others. When addicts do this, they are able to ask others about the harm they have done to them and also able to ask for forgiveness and make amends.

Sex addicts must stop trying to please others at all costs. Instead of manipulating people to get their needs met, addicts must learn to ask for what they need. They need to seek out supportive friends to help meet those needs. Friends are carefully chosen for their trustworthiness, ability to give constructive and caring advice, and their willingness to confront old behaviors if they should happen again. They must also be safe friends—friends who are not potential sexual partners. For this reason, heterosexuals may choose to have friendships only with people of the same sex.

To establish healthy relationships, the sex addict needs to establish healthy boundaries in those relationships. For example, the sex addict might say, "I will be honest with you and try not to hurt you. If I ever do anything that causes you harm, please let me know. I never intend to be sexual with you. Sometimes I don't realize my old behaviors. Please let me know if I do something that is inappropriate."

Recovering sex addicts also need to learn how to play. They generally have forgotten how to play, perhaps because of their abuse. They may be workaholics, or have a hard time playing because they believe it is a "waste of time." Playing may remind them of their abusive childhood. Yet play is a vital element of healthy relationships. Recovery is not all pain and blackness. It is about enjoying life and the world God has given. Most adults think of playing adult games or sports when they think of play. Play, however, could mean relearning how a child would play. I encourage some clients to go to a toy store and buy themselves something they always wanted as a child. This may sound a bit trite, but addicts are searching for joy and spontaneity and sometimes a toy can help them rediscover these things.

Codependency

When sex addicts achieve a certain level of sobriety—anytime between the sixth and ninth month—the pain of loneliness and the fear of losing friends and family hits them.

The anxiety of codependency can be frightening. Sex addicts who are married, for example, will be afraid their spouse will leave them. In the initial recovery period, spouses may be supportive, but when they sense that the sex addict is safely recovering, they may allow their own feelings to surface. This experience intensifies the sex addict's fear of abandonment.

As their behaviors become known, sex addicts are also afraid of losing others. This includes children, friends, extended family members, church friends, and coworkers. Recovering sex addicts battle the fear that if people really knew them, they would leave. During this time they need extra support from faithful friends.

Healing anxiety and fear is ultimately a spiritual challenge. Learning to trust God is one of the keys to overcoming codependency.

Slips and Relapse

One of the major questions that spouses and others have is whether or not the addict will act out again after the healing journey has begun.

Often the words *slip* or *relapse* are used to describe this. A *slip* is when a sex addict acts out once, while a *relapse* is a series of acting-out behaviors. Slips and relapses are more likely to happen, if they do, six to twelve months after recovery starts. During this time there are four basic dangers. These are not necessarily progressive and can occur simultaneously.

Complacency

When addicts achieve a certain amount of sobriety, they start to think they can relax, that they have the problem under control. They may stop going to meetings, stop practicing healthy boundaries and discipline boundaries, and not practice other recovery strategies.

Painful Feelings

As addicts recover, they begin to experience more painful feelings because they are no longer medicated by their addiction. These feelings are extremely threatening to most addicts, and they will be tempted to turn to their sexual behaviors to find relief.

Weariness

Sex addicts start to get tired of being labeled an addict. They also grow tired of strict prohibitions on ritual behaviors. They want to be "normal," and relax or abandon their boundaries.

Consequences

Addicts have to face difficult consequences, such as monetary struggles or loss of employment. They are discouraged that their recovery does not prevent or solve these problems. This sense of futility brings with it the temptation to act out again.

When addicts slip, they need to take stock of themselves before they go into relapse. A slip means something in the recovery process has gone wrong. Addicts may have relaxed their boundaries, neglected meeting with a sponsor, or may be avoiding a painful emotion. With the help of others, addicts should pinpoint what went wrong and avoid that mistake in the future. Remember the Nehemiah principle that addicts must always use times of strength to prepare for times of weakness. Slips can teach us about weaknesses that weren't fully understood before.

When addicts make a slip or even when they go into relapse, it is not productive to beat themselves up too harshly, or the resulting feelings of shame can drive them back into the acting-out cycle. Rather, they should use the slip to learn something about their recovery.

Many sex addicts with long periods of sobriety slip up several times in the early days of their recovery. Gradually, the recovery program takes root and addicts learn to anticipate "slippery" times and places more readily. They are then able to put preventive measures in place.

The process of recovery is a strange one. It feels frightening and uncomfortable to sex addicts, and they may rebel against it. But as time goes on, the serenity of the program begins to set in. What was once unfamiliar becomes second nature, and they embrace the process as a lifesaver.

Spirituality

The process of recovery is a spiritual journey. In the early days of recovery, addicts experience the joy of the spiritual journey, but in the days and years to come the serenity of the journey deepens. The greatest challenge is to accept that healing is not a one-time experience of deliverance, but is a daily experience grounded in healthy decisions.

Deepening spirituality and recovery from sexual addiction are intertwined. Both involve healing individuals, healing relationships, surrendering to God, and daily commitment and discipline. Most of all, recovery and spirituality bring hope—hope for healing, hope for peace and serenity, hope for life changes, hope for new awareness, and hope for a deeper relationship with God.

Developing a Vision

Sex addicts must develop a vision. A vision is a clear idea of God's calling, plan, and purpose for one's life. It is a picture of where we want to go with our lives. If we don't know where we're going, we can't get there. The Bible says that people without vision perish (Proverbs 29:18).[5]

When the addicts develop a sense of their true calling, their vision, they have a much easier time staying sober. Everything they do falls in line with achieving higher goals. Here are examples of vision statements for sex addicts:

- I seek to serve *God +* my spouse and not hurt her anymore.
- I want to share the message of hope and sobriety with other men who still struggle.
- I want my children to be raised in a safer home than I was.
- I hope to be able to repay all the money I spent on my addiction.
- I seek to make amends to those I've harmed.

This is not an exhaustive list. Notice that these vision statements help strengthen a resolve to stay sober. In my own experience, the vision of no longer hurting my wife kept me from acting out countless times.

Vision statements become the foundation for outlining specific strategies. Marvin's vision was to share his message of hope with others. He approached his pastor and asked if there were other men the pastor knew who struggled with sexual addiction. Marvin arranged meetings with these men and told his story. Later, these men planned a workshop at their church and brought in a speaker to address sexual purity. After the workshop, over fifty men signed up to be in a support group to stay sexually pure. Marvin's vision led to a dynamic ministry at this church. While he was pursuing it, it gave him the conviction and strength to stay sober so he could continue to be a witness to others.

Having a vision creates energy because it aligns us with God's purposes and enables us to find our true giftedness. Living out our vision may even include using the pain of past experiences to reach out, witness to, and help others. Paul says God is the Father of all compassion and comfort, "who comforts us in all our troubles, so that we can comfort those in any trouble" (2 Corinthians 1:4). Even those who have lost careers because of addiction may find that recovery opens the door to God's larger plan. In the early days of my recovery, if anyone had told me I would one day speak, teach, write, and counsel others all over the world, I would have thought they were completely crazy. These are the kinds of doors God opens when we seek his will in our lives.

I described above how fantasy is an attempt to meet needs and heal wounds by imagining false solutions. Vision, on the other hand, is imagining God's plan for our lives and finding that in so doing we legitimately meet our needs and heal our wounds.

THE CYCLE OF HEALING

The healing journey addresses and reverses each stage of the sexual addiction cycle (presented in chapter 4). The new cycle is illustrated below:

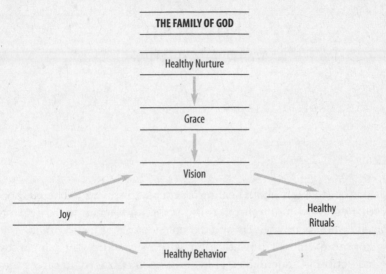

Figure 10: The Cycle of Healing

In the healthy cycle of healing, instead of unhealthy family dynamics, there is an experience of the family of God. Instead of wounds, there is healthy love and nurture. Instead of shame, there is grace. Understanding God's love, calling, plan, and purpose gives us a vision. Having a vision leads us into healthy rituals and discipline. Healthy rituals lead to healthy behavior. This kind of behavior brings us joy. Joy always feeds a vision.

A cycle builds on itself over and over again. It can be destructive, as with sexual addiction, or it can be constructive. As sex addicts constructively heal their broken lives, they are able to repair the damage they have done to others. For those who are married, there is no more important relationship than a spouse. The next chapter examines the healing process for couples.

HEALING
FOR COUPLES

I once began a talk about healing for couples by saying, "There is hope for couples who suffer from this disease." A woman there began to sob and wail uncontrollably and did not stop crying for an hour.

For those who are in relationship with a sex addict, the pain of sexual addiction is undeniable. They have been betrayed, deceived, and lied to. Their vows have been violated. They have been ignored or manipulated emotionally and physically. Their spouses may have asked them to engage in repulsive and abusive sexual practices. They have been placed in danger of sexually transmitted diseases. They have every right to be angry.

Despite the pain and anger, I still say there is hope for couples who have suffered from sexual addiction. I know because my wife, Deb, and I have been there. Marriages can be saved. Couples can rebuild trust and develop emotional, physical, and spiritual intimacy. This does not require spouses and addicts to deny their intense feelings, but it does require them to work through these feelings and even use them to build stronger relationships.

As I've said before, the work of healing may seem overwhelming. But both Deb and I can also affirm that it is worth all the work. We pray that God gives couples who go through the pain of sexual addiction a greater and deeper experience of intimacy than they have ever known before.

The phrase *sexually addicted couple* refers to a couple in which at least one person is a sex addict. The term *co-addict* refers to the spouse of a sex addict. The word *couple* generally means married couples, although unmarried couples can apply this material to their relationships as well.

This chapter covers essential elements of the healing journey for couples. When Deb and I had been in recovery for several years, we sat down and outlined key insights couples should know as they begin the healing journey. The bulk of this chapter is based on those insights. What follows is not a process that follows a straight line from start to finish; rather, it is a collection of ideas and strategies that are part of the ongoing journey. This chapter is divided into two parts. The first part consists of four issues that are critical in the early months of healing. The second part discusses issues that are important as the journey continues.

FOUR CRITICAL ISSUES IN THE EARLY MONTHS OF HEALING

Sexually Addicted Couples Should Try to Stay Together

The place to start is with a commitment to stay in the relationship by both addict and co-addict. This assumes the addict has gained and is maintaining sobriety. The biblical message is clear: a married couple becomes "one flesh." There are some in the recovery community who may be suspicious of this commitment because commitment to the relationship could be mistaken for *enmeshment*, a codependent phenomenon in which one person becomes so attached to another that his or her identity is consumed by the other person. The concern is that the Christian idea of oneness means that a spouse becomes a slave to his or her partner.

Spouses living with sex addicts might be enmeshed with the addict if they are not confronting the problem and demanding change. No doubt many Christian partners have enabled addictions by using misapplied Christian beliefs as part of their denial mechanism. However, serving and being faithful to partners means confronting them with their sinful behavior.

To stop enmeshment, some in the recovery community may encourage separation and even divorce. This may help individuals achieve sobriety, but it does nothing to help them with their relationships. A sexually addicted couple desperately needs to bring recovery to their entire relationship. If they need sponsors, meetings, and therapy as individuals, they also need sponsors, meetings, and therapy as a couple. The sponsor should be another couple with whom they can talk when they encounter couple issues. They need to go to support group meetings as a couple. Recovering Couples Anonymous was started for just such a purpose.[1] There are also Christian recovery groups for couples.

All of these meetings and therapies are time consuming and often expensive. Yet this kind of support is critical for the couple, particularly in the first year. The same kind of recovery that is undertaken for the individual addict must also be undertaken for the couple.

It may be courageous and mature for a partner to leave a sex addict to avoid enmeshment; however, it may be even more courageous and mature when a partner stays and works on the relationship. A co-addict may need to leave a relationship if the sex addict doesn't change and the relationship is emotionally or physically dangerous. However, two people can address the problem of enmeshment or codependency while living together. In fact, it might be better to practice taking care of oneself while in relationship. Addicts are good at running away from difficult relationships; sexually addicted couples in recovery need not make this mistake.

Here is a general principle to follow to assess whether or not your decision to stay in the relationship is based on enmeshment/codependency or on a healthy commitment to serve and remain in relationship with your partner. Codependents surrender to and serve their partners out of *weakness*. They are afraid to be alone and feel needy. Healthy partners surrender to and serve their partners out of *strength*. They are secure in themselves and know they could be alone. They choose to be in relationship.

For example, Jennifer's husband, Tim, had been a sex addict for years. She knew about much of his behavior their entire marriage. She was afraid to leave because she didn't feel she knew how to take care of herself. She put up with Tim's behaviors because she was afraid of being alone. Rather than face her fears, she masked them behind strong religious beliefs about the sanctity of marriage. When Tim heard about a support group at church for men struggling with sexual addiction and decided to join, Jennifer was thrilled. Tim challenged her to go to a similar support group for wives. Though she was hesitant at first, she eventually decided to attend. There she found a caring and supportive group of women who challenged her to learn how to care for and nurture herself. The women in the group offered her the freedom and grace to leave the relationship if she felt she needed to. As Jennifer grew stronger in her faith and her confidence in herself, she decided to stay in the relationship. When Tim had been sober for one year, he and Jennifer decided to reaffirm their wedding vows together.

Sexual Co-addicts Must Join the Healing Journey

The co-addict marries the sex addict. Contrary to what many people may think, spouses don't become co-addicts because they marry a sex addict. Marrying a sex addict is not an accident. Consciously or not, the partners of sex addicts intentionally chose their relationships. They may be abuse victims with codependency and/or intimacy disorders. Some sexual co-addicts are bashful or inhibited about sex. They believe if they marry a sex addict, they will have a good sex life because they never have to initiate—the sex addict always will.

Co-addicts may assume that when the sex addict gets into recovery, all of their troubles will be over. They may think their problems are due solely to the sexual acting out and when that stops all other difficulties will stop. The problem is that they expect the sex addict to do all the work of recovery. It is vitally important for sexual co-addicts to look at themselves and not put all the responsibility for relationship healing on the sex addict. The co-addict needs to be in recovery too.

Next to forgiveness, the greatest gift my wife, Deb, has given me is the gift of looking at her own wounds and issues. From the start, Deb chose to go to counseling for herself, to go to counseling with me, and to understand that the dysfunction in our relationship was independent of my sexual addiction. I've heard her say many times that sexual addiction didn't cause our problems. My sexual sins certainly made things worse, but they were only one problem I brought into our marriage. Sexual acting out was one expression of how I coped with my loneliness.

After seventeen years of sobriety, Deb trusts me. However, she feels that trust isn't really the central issue in our relationship. She tells many audiences and clients that we are all sinners and we all make many mistakes. Now, if either one of us makes mistakes, we first ask what part of our healing journey has broken down such that there is distance between us. When there is distance, either one of us might be tempted to cope in old ways.

Sexually Addicted Couples Must Take Mutual Responsibility for the Disease of Their Relationship

When both members of a sexually addicted relationship see the need to heal, they have accepted that they are mutually responsible. This does not mean the co-addict is responsible for the behaviors of the sex addict. Neither does it mean the sex addict is responsible for any unhealthy behaviors of the co-addict. It does mean they both are responsible for the state of their relationship.

One trait of unhealthy family dynamics is that partners blame each other and don't take responsibility for their own problems. Most conversations start with the words, "You always," or "You never." In healthy relationships, however, conversations begin with "I think," or "I feel," or "I take responsibility for the fact that . . . "

One exercise sexually addicted couples can practice is called the "couple's personal inventory." First on a daily basis and later on a weekly basis, couples take fifteen minutes by themselves and make two lists. One list is entitled, "The things you did today (or this week) that were helpful to me or to our relationship." The second list is, "The things I did that were not helpful to you or to our relationship." The couple then exchanges lists. They ask questions for clarification, but they are not to add to each other's lists. Comments like "You forgot that I . . . " or "You forgot when you . . . " are not allowed.

This exercise forces the couple to stop blaming each other, to take responsibility for their own behavior, to affirm their partner, and to start educating each other on what they like. If sexually addicted couples can accept mutual responsibility for the disease of the relationship, then they can take the first step of Recovering Couples Anonymous: "We admitted we are powerless over our relationship and that our life together has become unmanageable."

The co-addict must realize that he or she is not responsible for the sexual sobriety of the addict. Sex addicts are responsible for their own recovery and for setting their own boundaries. Questions like, "Should you be watching that?" or "Should you be going to that place?" only remind addicts of old behavior and memories. Sex addicts must be responsible for their own behaviors if they are to recover.

To build trust, sex addicts need to treat their spouse with consistency and caring. They should maintain trust by calling when they will be late, explaining any behavior that may seem questionable, and being considerate of their partner's feelings. One sex addict was watching his kids at the bowling alley when a woman approached him and struck up a conversation about bowling and the kids. When his wife discovered them talking together, she was enraged. Instead of accusing her of not trusting him, the man said, "I can see that this scene would remind you of my past behaviors. That must really hurt." Because he allowed her to have her feelings, she felt heard, accepted, and cared for.

Members of Sexually Addicted Couples Must Confront Their Own Abuse

According to Pat Carnes's research, four out of every five sex addicts have been sexually abused, three out of every four have been physically abused, and almost all of them have been emotionally abused. Carnes also found that those who are married to sex addicts have virtually the same incidence of abuse.[2]

What are we to make of this? Abuse victims seem to find each other. For example, a man who has been abandoned by his mother may search for a woman to nurture him in a motherly way. He may find a woman whose father abandoned her and who needs to please a man in order to get the attention and nurturing she never had. The obvious problem is that no one, not even a marriage partner, can take the place of a parent. When it becomes obvious that his wife isn't going to mother him, the husband may be enraged.

For couples, these dynamics can be extremely painful and lead to more addictive behavior. For example, the spouse of an abuse victim might say something that triggers the victim of abuse to kick into "survival" mode, becoming distant, angry, or addictive. The spouse, in turn, reacts by being angry or distant. And, in a continuing downward spiral, the victim of abuse looks for further escapes from his or her spouse, creating an addictive cycle of its own (see figure 11 on the next page).

In recovery, addicts realize that abuse issues belong to parents or other perpetrators, not to the spouse. Making this distinction takes pressure off of the spouse and facilitates greater intimacy. Spouses abandoned as children need to grieve the loss of the parent who abandoned them. When they work on these emotions, spouses stop trying to get parental nurture from their partners. This frees partners to provide the care and nurture of a marriage partner rather than a parent.

Today, my wife and I firmly believe that even though husbands and wives may have found each other out of woundedness, God can redeem this dynamic as part of his providence and design. Two wounded people have the potential to be either enemies, blaming each other for their pain, or allies and companions on the journey of healing. In working with hundreds of couples we have seen that one partner's strength may be another partner's weakness. This means that most couples have matched sets of strengths and weaknesses.

Michael came from a religious family that did not think about money or plan for financial stability. Michael doesn't worry about money, but he is a terrible financial manager. Mary came from a family that was not very religious, but managed money very well. Mary worries about money but really knows how to save and invest it. Michael and Mary fought over money for years. Michael hated Mary's "obsession" with money and her criticism of him; Mary hated Michael's "irresponsibility" and criticism of her. Michael and Mary discovered that they had a matched set of strengths and weaknesses. Michael could teach Mary about faith and serenity about money, and Mary could teach Michael about managing it. Before they had been enemies, now they are allies.

This dynamic goes deeper. When a couple honestly shares hurts from the past, they can connect through mutual pain and grieving. They can empathize with and support each other. Couples who connect in this way also know that they can participate in the journey of healing with Christ, who shares their pain. These couples become yoked with Jesus and experience a much lighter burden.

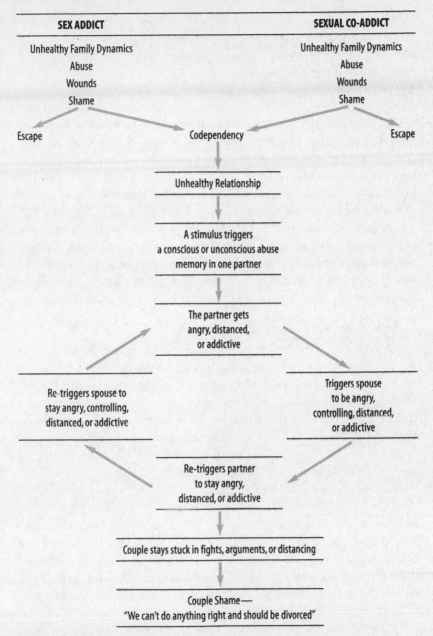

SEX ADDICT

SEXUAL CO-ADDICT

Unhealthy Family Dynamics
Abuse
Wounds
Shame

Unhealthy Family Dynamics
Abuse
Wounds
Shame

Escape

Codependency

Escape

Unhealthy Relationship

A stimulus triggers
a conscious or unconscious abuse
memory in one partner

The partner gets
angry, distanced,
or addictive

Re-triggers spouse to
stay angry, controlling,
distanced, or addictive

Triggers spouse
to be angry,
controlling, distanced,
or addictive

Re-triggers partner
to stay angry,
distanced, or addictive

Couple stays stuck in fights, arguments, or distancing

Couple Shame—
"We can't do anything right and should be divorced"

Figure 11: Addiction Cycle for Couples

IMPORTANT ISSUES FOR THE ONGOING JOURNEY OF HEALING

Sexually Addicted Couples Must Strive Toward Intimacy

Most sexually addicted couples have intimacy disorders because they believe "no one will like me as I am. If you knew me, you would hate me and you would leave me." Intimacy implies vulnerability and a willingness to let at least one other person know who you really are, what you think, and what you feel. Sex addicts can't experience this kind of intimacy for fear of being abandoned.

Intimacy disorder is one of the hardest parts of recovery. When trust is repeatedly violated, it becomes extremely difficult to break through the feelings of anger and resentment. To build intimacy, couples need to talk about past sexual behaviors, learn how to have safe conversations about anger and resentment, and discover how to play together.

1. Talk about Past Sexual Behaviors

One challenge is determining how much information sex addicts should tell their partners about past sexual behaviors. Some tell all by blurting it out to get it over with. Others fear their spouses will leave if certain facts come out. The latter group often "practices" telling the truth. They tell part of it and wait for the reaction. If the spouse doesn't leave, they tell more of the truth. This process may go on for days, weeks, or months. The spouse might begin to wonder, "When am I going to know the whole story?" and feel the addict is still lying.

Recovering sex addicts may not want to deceive or lie anymore, but they fear being abandoned. They may also not want to hurt their spouse by revealing specific details. Recovery for sex addicts and spouses means both partners have to take risks to tell and hear the truth. After years of being deceived and wondering about the truth, spouses may be relieved to hear the whole story. Later, the relief may wear off as the pain of the facts sinks in. In recovery, couples need to give each other permission to talk about these feelings whenever they surface.

Intimacy disorder is overcome only when both partners decide to risk telling who they really are, how they feel, and what they think. A couple must practice truth-telling daily. Practice may start with insignificant material and, as the couple gets more comfortable with the process of talking, progress to more significant material.

There must be some level of truth-telling. Sex addicts can't spend the rest of their lives wondering about whether their spouse will find out. Spouses can't spend the rest of their lives wondering what they will find out. The broad outline of sexual acting out should be told, but not necessarily the specifics.

Before talking, the sex addict should ask, "Why do I want to tell? What do I expect to accomplish by telling this?" When listening, the spouse of the sex addict should ask, "Why do I want to know?" Truth-telling must always take place to build intimacy, not to control feelings and behaviors or to punish. Intimacy results when truth is told for the right reasons and when it clears up old confusions about what was really going on.

There are also times when it becomes a moral imperative to tell the truth. Tom was a missionary in Africa. For years, at the time when AIDS was rapidly spreading, he had unprotected sex with prostitutes. During the same time, he continued to have sex with his wife. It is morally imperative that he tell her the truth so she can be tested for AIDS and other sexually transmitted diseases. Marvin told countless lies to his wife to create opportunities for him to act out and to cover his sins afterward. It is morally imperative for him to tell his wife so she won't be confused and can adjust her sense of reality. Betty had an affair with her husband's best friend. In this case, she must tell her husband the specific truth so he can make his own decision about that friendship.

2. Learn to Have Safe Conversations about Anger and Resentment

For a relationship to be successful, couples need to let each other know about anger, resentment, and behaviors they don't like. I encourage them to draw up a "safety contract" that dictates how they may communicate fairly by expressing their anger in healthy ways. Doing this begins to change old patterns of fighting into new patterns of healthy intimacy. When my wife and I express anger to each other in safe ways, it can be one of the most intimate things we do.

First, couples list their destructive fighting strategies. Such a list might include name-calling, profanity, rehashing past behaviors to prove a point (sometimes called "case building"), using "you" statements, fighting in front of children, fighting after 10 p.m., using violence, and so on. The list clearly details where couples have failed in the past.

The couple can now define the contract, listing rules they will follow in the future: We won't name-call, use profanity, use violence, fight in front of the kids, and so on. The contract must provide safety so each partner feels comfortable about expressing his or her feelings. The contract may contain time boundaries, such as we will fight for only thirty minutes, we can take time-outs, we can continue or reschedule fights, and we don't have to resolve the issue we are fighting about.

Couples who don't fight, at least historically, still need to express their feelings. They can set a time out each week to meet together. Before they get to this "fight," they make a list of things that angered or hurt them that week. During the conversation, they simply read their list, prefacing it with reassuring statements like, "This list is about my feelings; it is not about wanting to get divorced," or "This list is about your behaviors and not about you," or "I need you to know I still love you, but this list is about behaviors I don't like." The key element is safety. The rules of the contract take effect whenever a fight starts. If rules are violated, one partner will not feel safe and can get away from the fight if he or she needs to. In recovery, other couples, a sponsor, a counselor, or a pastor must monitor these contracts.

3. Play Together

Sexually addicted couples have forgotten (or never knew) how to play together. These couples need to be disciplined about play, setting aside time together to do activities they enjoy. The play can be silly or sophisticated, ranging from building a snowman to going to an art gallery. One couple decided to decorate their yard for Christmas. The man hung lights; the woman put designs on a large wooden snowman. They transformed their front yard into a festive playland, and the neighborhood loved it. We often advise couples who want to learn more about how to play to observe how children play. The kids could be their own, their grandchildren, or (as one couple did) children at Sunday school. In order to try some of the ideas you see, you might have to encourage each other to be uninhibited. Deb and I remembered how much we liked to swing when we were kids, so we sometimes still do that today.

Sexually Addicted Couples Need to Heal Their Sexual Relationship

The subject of building intimacy in marriage through sex deserves a book in itself. The following are highlights of areas sexually addicted couples need to examine in their sexual relationship.

Early in recovery, sex addicts need to observe a period of celibacy in order to reverse the belief that sex is their most important need. They also need to learn that sex is not an indicator of whether or not a spouse loves them. Spouses need to learn that sex is not always the way they please their partner. Abstinence takes the sexual pressure off the relationship so the couple can work on play and communication.

Throughout the healing journey, a couple may want to be celibate at other times in order to center themselves emotionally and spiritually. Other times for celibacy include when a spouse needs to confront childhood abuse. Celibacy contracts can require that sex happen only under certain safe conditions and in certain ways.

Sex addicts need to establish boundaries for themselves, promising not to fantasize about other partners during sex and promising not to use sex as an escape from feelings. If the sex addict feels lonely, tired, angry, or afraid, this is not a time to be sexual.

Sex addicts must learn to be sexual as an expression of their emotional and spiritual feelings for their partners. At first this understanding of sex may not be as exciting because it lacks adrenaline or danger, but it can be more fulfilling.

The couple may need to get some basic sexual information. Some couples, even those in which the addict had had 500 different partners, didn't know basic sexual information. They should consult their doctors and counselors or read books on sexuality. (See the Resources section on page 228.)

Some sexually addicted couples experience sexual dysfunction, impotence, inhibition, or premature ejaculation. These problems may be strictly physical; for example, impotence can be caused by diabetic complications. Or they can be psychological; for example, incest wounds can impair a person's ability to get sexually excited. Since it is likely that both partners are sexual abuse victims, they may have a very difficult time with positive sexual expression. In these cases the couple can seek the help of a counselor who knows how to work through these problems.

The couple must learn how to express sexual likes and dislikes. Sexual co-addicts may never have talked about what they like. Doing so sometimes involves shame or embarrassment and could take lots of practice.

The couple must be good at self-nurture. A healthy sexual relationship can only occur if both people like themselves as well as each other. Self-nurture involves giving oneself affirmation. It means each one takes care of his or her own emotional, physical, and spiritual needs.

For example, one woman never wanted to have sex with her husband, the sex addict, because she felt physically unattractive. No matter how many times he told her she was attractive to him, she wouldn't believe it because she thought he was just lying to get her to be sexual. Until this wife accepts her own body, she won't be able to share it with her husband comfortably or experience mutual enjoyment.

If the couple can work on these things, they develop a wonderful sexual intimacy. One couple told me that, after their first experience of nonaddictive sex, they both held each other and cried for joy. They experienced the difference between addicted sex and fulfilling sex. Instead of being in a fantasyland, for the first time they enjoyed themselves together, for who they were.

Sexually Addicted Couples Must Deal with Codependency Issues

Sexually addicted couples are often two codependent people living together. The demanding partner uses the sacrificial partner to get his or her own way. When the sacrificial person starts to stand up for his or her rights, the demanding partner may feel threatened.

For example, one recovering sex addict had achieved about eighteen months of sobriety when his wife decided she would get inpatient treatment for the abuse she experienced as a child. When she left for treatment, her husband felt tremendously anxious she would never come back to him. He reported that this period of anxiety was as great or greater than anything he experienced during his time of sexual acting out.

The honesty required to have a healthy relationship is blocked by codependency. Codependency and intimacy disorders are related. Christians who seek relationship and intimacy can enlist the aid of their faith. Couples without a shared faith should consider pursuing a spiritual path together to find it. Jesus said we must be willing to lose our life in order to get it back, and the same is true of marriage. Surrendering our marriage to Christ means we are willing to live without it. This frightens sex addicts and their spouses. But when they come to accept that God will care for them and they can survive alone, then they have the freedom to be honest about their feelings and can share personal information about who they really are.

Sexually Addicted Couples Must Overcome Their Shame

Sexually addicted couples are ashamed. Not only are they ashamed individually, but also as a couple because of codependency and intimacy disorders. Couple shame makes them feel that they have a bad marriage and that people won't want to associate with them. One recovering couple recently moved into a new neighborhood. When their neighbors didn't immediately come over to introduce themselves, this couple was convinced the whole neighborhood knew about their sexual addiction.

Couple shame makes the couple feel they are bad parents. It taunts them with thoughts like, "We don't have a nice house, we don't take care of our money, and we fight too much." Ultimately couple shame tells the couple that the only solution to this terrible marriage is divorce.

Couples need to find groups and other couples to talk to who show them they are not alone. They need to know other couples have similar behaviors and that they are still accepted despite their worst behaviors. Shame diminishes when there is a network of couples providing the support necessary for the relationship to survive.

Sexually Addicted Couples Need to Heal Their Image of the Ideal Relationship

Almost all couples have an idea of the perfect marriage. Sexually addicted couples have to bury, reclaim, or adjust their ideals because they have been repeatedly violated or were unrealistic in the first place. For example, almost all couples vow to be faithful to each other when they are married. Most sexually addicted couples have experienced major violations of this vow. Some couples expect to have a certain house, a certain type of family, or a certain amount of money in the bank. Either the addiction or circumstances or both have prevented attaining these ideals.

Some sexually addicted couples operate with unrealistic Christian images. One couple focused on the idea of never letting the sun set on their anger (Ephesians 4:26). They talked, argued, and fought into the middle of the night, long past sunset, trying to get things straight. The sex addict would not be satisfied until his wife had forgiven him, agreed with him, or made up. All the wife wanted was to escape, be by herself, and get away from his incessant talking and demands.

I encourage sexually addicted couples to make a list defining the ideal couple: They never commit adultery, they have lots of money, their kids are perfect, and so on. Then the couple asks themselves which items on the list they have violated. Before they get too down on themselves, they should ask more questions. First, which ideals are realistic? Unrealistic ideals should be discarded. For example, couples might say, "We give ourselves permission not to have the best house in the neighborhood."

Second, which ideals can be restored? It is realistic to be sexually faithful in marriage. This is a positive Christian value. Many sexually addicted couples renew their marriage vows, sometimes in the presence of a minister.

Finally, which ideals can be achieved with help? For example, a couple may want to attain financial stability and decide to consult a financial adviser to help set budgets, suggest solutions, and monitor progress.

Sexually addicted couples may never become the ideal couple they once imagined, but with help they can salvage their relationship and build a marriage based on realistic goals and worthy ideals.

Sexually Addicted Couples Must Beware of Reverting to Old Patterns of Behavior

Awhile back I tried to help my son correct his tennis swing. The correction allowed him to hit the ball harder and more accurately. He complained, however, that it felt weird and it hurt. Of course it did. It was unfamiliar because he was using muscles in a new way. Later, I discovered him practicing with someone else and hitting the ball the same old way. It didn't work as well, but it felt better.

Healing is much the same. New behaviors and healthy choices work better and produce healthy results, but they often "hurt." They don't feel familiar, they are scary, and they take lots of work. Healing is hard work and is painful at times even though it produces joy and serenity and health.

Sexually addicted couples in recovery will experience new intimacy in their relationship, but it is unfamiliar. We are creatures of habit and of comfort. If we learned destructive patterns growing up, those are familiar, and we may unconsciously revert to them at times.

Sexually addicted couples must be aware of the temptation to revert to old patterns. What was normal for them may have been fighting, deception, adultery, silence, coldness, sexual unavailability, and endless other forms of craziness. Sometimes this craziness might seem more normal and even safer than newer intimacies.

The early days of recovery, when the couple experiences new honesty and relationship, must be followed up with great discipline and care. Recovery is not a constantly wonderful progression. Old patterns will reoccur. This should not be interpreted as failure, but as a sign of the difficulty of the journey.

Sexually Addicted Couples Should Not Expect Social Support for Their Recovery

Just as recovery is unfamiliar for the couple, so it is for those around them. Families (even children), work associates, and old friends may not support the recovery process. They may not understand it or agree with it. They may not like the new honesty or changed behaviors because it makes them uncomfortable with their own way of living. And they may simply like things better the old way.

Thus, sexually addicted couples may encounter resistance to the changes they want to make. A brother of a sex addict asked, "When are we going to be a normal family again?" The addict said, "Never! Normal is crazy." The brother was extremely angry and still hasn't talked to the addict.

A female alumni of our ministry appeared on a television show, and even though she wore a disguise, someone at church recognized her. Eventually, the pastor asked her to leave the church because of objections at church.

Sexually addicted couples have to be strong in the face of misunderstanding, judgment, and hostility. They need to establish new support networks. Ultimately, they might have to move, change jobs, or not see their families for a while. The couple may need to grieve the loss of many relationships. This is very painful, but could be necessary to stay in recovery.

Sexually Addicted Couples Who Don't Work on Their Relationship Will Repeat the Same Mistakes in the Next

Sometimes the pain, shame, sadness, and anger are so intense, a sexually addicted couple may think the only solution is to get divorced. They may think, "I made a mistake and found the wrong partner. This is not the person God really chose for me. I still need to find him or her." They think that with a new husband or wife all their problems will disappear.

One sexually addicted couple met each other after recovery. He had been in recovery from sexual addiction for five years, she from alcoholism for ten years. They assumed that since they were in recovery individually, their relationship would be easy. In the early days it was exciting and wonderful. However, several months into the marriage the honeymoon wore off and old issues from previous marriages returned. They asked themselves, "How could this new person be so much like my old partner?"

The reason is that they probably chose someone just like their old partner. They learned how to make this selection in their family of origin. Even though they were both in individual recovery, their relationship experienced old problems. The healing of relationships needs to happen while a person is in a relationship. You can't practice relationship issues by yourself.

I am not suggesting that a couple should stay married at all costs. As a Christian, I believe strongly in marriage, but not every marriage succeeds. If one person is getting beaten up physically or emotionally, he or she might need to get out. Even a sex addict might need to separate if the spouse can't get into recovery, forgive, and work on healing the relationship. However, it is important to understand that getting out of one relationship does not bring success in the next. Many people have been married several times, and each marriage is a carbon copy of the last one.

The healing journey for couples is a daily challenge, yet there is great hope of success. The wounds of the past do heal. With God's help and the support of others, couples can find new joy.

Sexually Addicted Couples Should Be Considerate of Their Children

One of the most frequent questions sexually addicted couples ask is, "What should we tell the children?" Depending on their age, children should be told that Dad or Mom is getting help for sexual addiction and that sexual addiction is about not being able to stop sexual behaviors outside of marriage. Most of all, children need to know that Mom and Dad intend to stay together and that they, the children, will be safe. In early recovery, parents should hold family meetings to let the children know in simple terms what is going on. Parents should explain the changes that will ensue, such as meetings the parents have to attend, or having to move to a new location.

As they communicate to their children, sexually addicted couples need to model for children how to express their feelings. They should not share their feelings to get sympathy or support from their children, for that is emotional incest. The children should see, however, that their parents have feelings, are dealing with them, and are making healthier choices.

Kids are extremely resilient and understanding if parents are honest with them. Being frank about sexual sins gives parents the chance to talk about sexual morality with credibility. They are being honest. They know what they are talking about. It also allows children the chance to come to their parents when they need to make tough sexual choices.

Many sexually addicted couples recognize that they have harmed their children and look for ways to make amends. A parent may say, "I'm sorry I have been angry with you lately. This anger is not your fault. And it doesn't mean I don't love you. I was working through some issues in my life, and I took my anger about them out on you. I'll try not to do it again." The parent might also say, "If you ever feel I am doing something to you that is not fair, please come directly to me and we will talk about it."

In ways like this, the parent teaches the children to take responsibility for behavior. The parent also shows children they are loved and that they don't deserve unfair treatment. As children learn to take responsibility, make healthy choices, and not allow themselves to be abused, the chain of addiction in a family system is broken.

I have asked myself, if my parents had chosen to be honest with me about their struggles, would I have respected them more or less? My answer is that I would have felt less lonely if I'd known I was not the only one who was struggling. To know that my own parents made mistakes and that they knew how to deal with them in a healthy way would have been a great blessing.

Today, Deb and I have many great conversations with our children I never would have dreamed of having with my parents. That is a blessing for me and I hope it is for them as well.

Sexually Addicted Couples Can Grow Together Spiritually

The greatest miracle of recovery is a deepening relationship with God. As sex addicts grow individually, they must bring their spiritual growth to their partners and learn how to grow together spiritually as a couple. In early recovery, the sexually addicted couple can establish a "spiritual quest" contract, pledging to go to church together, pray and read Scripture together, or have family devotions. The contract should be monitored by Christian friends, a support network, or the couple's pastor.

Couples must be aware that either partner could be a spiritual abuse victim. If so, participating in any religious practice may remind them of past pain. One sex addict, a minister's son, was sexually and emotionally abused by his father and was forced to be at church many hours every week. All of these dynamics make it very hard for him to go into a church building. For years he was unable to tell his wife why he didn't want to go to church. Without that information she believed he didn't care, and her anger only drove him farther away from church.

A spiritual contract helps a couple to build trust. They commit to each other and to God to be honest and faithful to each other. Sometimes, to seal this vow, a couple officially rededicates their marriage vows in a ceremony. This spiritual contract should include spiritual discipline and the commitment to pray together, study Scripture, and participate in a worshiping community. A spiritual contract can only proceed when there have been three acts of surrender:

1. The husband and wife must surrender their own lives to Christ.
2. The husband and wife must surrender each other's lives to Christ. Neither one of them has any power to control the other and must trust that all of a partner's actions are between him or her and God.
3. The husband and wife must surrender their marriage to Christ. They are powerless without God's help.

Finally, a couple needs to have a vision together as a couple. So many couples can be divided by pursuing individual visions. If I have a vision of my calling and Deb has a vision of her calling, what we really have is two visions and most probably division. If I pursue mine and Deb hasn't fully embraced it, when I go off to pursue it she may be resentful. It has given us a great deal of joy to ask God the simple question, "What is your calling, plan, and purpose for us as a couple?"

Couples who can develop a vision agree to become allies in the journey. We live in a culture that has been, and continues to be, wounded by divorce and broken families. Sexually addicted couples who survive their pain and rebuild their marriages have much to teach us about the joys of becoming one flesh, breaking the cycle of abuse, and rebuilding families. Sexually addicted couples who choose to heal their relationships and build new and healthier ones break the cycle of sins that have been passed down, as the Bible says, for generations.

PART IV

HEALING THE WOUNDS OF THE CHURCH

CHAPTER 12

SEXUALLY ADDICTED PASTORS AND PRIESTS[1]

As a twelve-year-old boy, Peter was sexually molested by a man in a public park. When he told his local priest in the confessional, the priest wanted to hear explicit details and eventually persuaded Peter to perform the same acts with him.

As a young man, Peter engaged in anonymous sexual activity with other men. He sought to stop the behavior, but his career led him to many places where sexual connections were easy. Eventually, he decided to enter the priesthood, thinking he could alleviate his sense of shame by joining himself to God and that people would respect him if he were a "father" to them. He also hoped his vow of celibacy would keep him from further acting out.

This was not to be the case. In seminary, his homosexual acting out continued with classmates and progressively became more active. Later, as a parish priest, he seduced altar boys and boys from the youth group who were the same age he was when first molested. Finally, Peter was arrested. Fortunately for him, he was able to get treatment for sexual addiction.

Sexual sins, like the ones Peter committed, cause great pain to members of the church. We must understand the characteristics of sexually addicted clergy. Healing the church and its members can only begin when pastors are able to deal with their secret sins and heal their own wounds. As leaders, they possess the spiritual authority to model healing.

Pastors tend to be placed on pedestals and are expected to be perfectly spiritual. They are a symbol to others that it is possible to have faith. When they commit sin it is very threatening. Observers might wonder, "If a minister can fall this badly, what hope is there for me to avoid committing such sins?"

A WIDESPREAD PROBLEM

The problem of pastoral sexual misconduct is a large one. As I said earlier, in one study, 40 percent of all pastors confessed to problems with pornography. A *Leadership Journal* survey revealed that 23 percent of 300 pastors had done something sexually inappropriate with someone other than their spouse.[2] Furthermore, 12 percent of pastors had engaged in intercourse with people other than their spouse. Tim LaHaye noticed that, at one point, the churches of the city of Dallas all seemed under attack because so many pulpits were vacated by sexual disgrace.[3] Nationally known evangelists have brought large-scale media attention to this problem. Most Christians are aware of at least one pastor who has "fallen" because of sexual sin.

Our legal system is also forcing the church to look seriously at pastoral sexual misconduct. Hundreds of victims have filed civil lawsuits against pastors and priests for the emotional damage created by sexual abuse and exploitation. Some victims have even sued whole denominations for keeping situations quiet and for transferring clergy. As one Catholic bishop told me, "It used to be that when a priest committed sexual misconduct, we kept it as quiet as possible. We tried to control the damage, and we transferred the priest. We can no longer get away with that." The scandals in the Roman Catholic Church reached a boiling point in 2001, forcing the church to ask for the resignation of at least one cardinal and bringing bishops all over the United States under increasing scrutiny. This has led to "zero tolerance" policies. The saddest effect, however, is the damage done to the laity's faith and trust. Church hierarchy has been more concerned with protecting the church than with exposing the truth and making restitution to victims.

CONTRIBUTORS TO PASTORAL SEXUAL VULNERABILITY

There are three primary contributors to pastoral sexual vulnerability. First, there is the pastor's personal responsibility. Second, there is the responsibility of the system, or the family, of the local church. We know that, just like unhealthy marriages, an unhealthy pastor may get connected with an unhealthy church. Finally, there is the system of the larger church nationally or internationally.

The Pastor

Whatever the circumstances, pastoral sexual misconduct is the pastor's responsibility. Even if a person has pursued the pastor and tried to seduce him or her, it is still the pastor's responsibility to refuse, just as Joseph refused Potiphar's wife (Genesis 39).

In his book *The Wounded Healer*, pastoral psychologist Henri Nouwen characterizes pastors as caring people who are often wounded by the sins, hurts, and burdens of their people; by their workload; and by loneliness. If they take care of themselves by getting help and support when they need it, they can grow stronger and wiser and become more compassionate and effective healers. Thus they become "wounded healers," true shepherds of both themselves and others.

But some ministers don't know how to care for their own wounds. They remain lonely, resentful, burned out, and angry. When they are not healed themselves, they are likely to injure others as they search for nurture, for ways to express their anger, and for ways to escape their feelings. Gil Gustafson, a former priest of the Archdiocese of Minneapolis and St. Paul, calls these pastors "unhealed wounders."

Pastors and priests who don't take time to heal their wounds damage their ministries and may cause harm to those they serve. When I was in seminary, I had many wounds I wasn't consciously aware of. My heart was to serve the church, but my unhealed wounds led me to selfish sexual acts. It would have been possible for me to receive the help, guidance, and education I needed early on in my training. In those days, however, the church didn't fully understand sexual abuse and addiction.

Today, we can do a much better job in helping candidates for ministry prepare for their work so they don't become unhealed wounders.

The Congregation

Church members tend to look to pastors with respect and devotion. We give pastors spiritual authority and we trust them. In many ways we look on them as we would a parent: We seek their pastoral love and approval and want to benefit from their spirituality.

Some church members are simply attracted to the pastor. He or she is powerful and charismatic, gentle and understanding. Whether a pastor is physically attractive or not, there can be a sexual energy in this attraction.

Some church members have been sexually abused as children. They learned to get approval from their parents through being sexual. If these people view their pastors as parents and need their approval, they might also think they need to be sexual with their pastors. When sex takes place between these people and their pastors, it is essentially incest, a parental figure being sexual with a childlike figure. Although it appears to be sex between two consenting adults, it is actually exploitative sex. Both sexual exploitation (sex between adults in which one adult uses the other) and sexual abuse (sex between an adult and a child) are punishable by law. In fact, pastors are serving jail terms for sexually exploiting their parishioners.

The Wider Church

Historically, the church has kept quiet about pastors who commit sexual immorality. In the past, a minister may have been defrocked, depending on the denomination, but more than likely the pastor simply left the church. Perhaps the pastor was transferred or found a new call. We tend to hope the geographic cure takes effect, repentance takes place, and sexual sinning stops. This seldom happens. Many pastors leave a trail of sexual misconduct behind them wherever they go.

The church may also assume that when a pastor has an affair, it is not the pastor's fault. Perhaps the pastor was under too much stress. Or perhaps the pastoral spouse is to blame for not taking care of the pastor's needs. Or the devil is to blame—maybe the devil pursues and tempts pastors more.

CHARACTERISTICS OF THE SEXUALLY ADDICTED PASTOR OR PRIEST

The following are characteristics of pastors and priests who struggle with sexual sin and addiction. Several of these characteristics are unique to clergy; others are similar to general characteristics of sexual addiction described in chapter 4. I have tried to delineate how these more general characteristics are uniquely expressed in pastoral and priestly roles.

Ordination as a Shame Reduction Strategy

The positional authority of pastors and priests often appeals to people with low self-esteem. They may (perhaps unconsciously) think, "I am a worthless person, but if I enter the ministry, people will like me, trust me, and think I'm worth something." A sex addict who is full of shame and wants to control his or her behaviors might also think, "If I become a pastor, my special relationship with God will change me, take away my lust, and protect me from sexual immorality."

Ruth entered the pastorate to escape the shame of her past. Molested and physically abused by a brother and her father, she found sanctuary in her church youth group. At age eighteen she went to college to escape her family. There she joined a campus church and, at one point, became sexually involved with the campus pastor.

Ruth then pursued physically abusive relationships. In some ways she encouraged this, even enjoying it, because violent sex had been "normal" to her as a child. However, her behavior also caused her deep shame.

Recognizing that her escape early in life had been through the church, Ruth decided more church involvement might give her a more permanent escape. She entered seminary and was eventually ordained. During a seminary internship, she discovered bars that connected people for the purpose of physically abusive sexual activity, and she allowed herself to be tied up and beaten on a regular basis. After she became a parish pastor, she drove into the city on her day off, her clerical garb providing good "cover" for the bruises she received.

After a while, Ruth wondered why her ordination hadn't "taken." She investigated ordination in another denomination. She was so depressed she sought the help of a therapist. Finally, this therapist recognized her sexual abuse and sexual addiction and convinced her to be treated. In treatment she realized she had expected her ordination to transform her. She thought her entire being would be different, that she would no longer desire to be physically beaten, and that lust would be taken away. She had been ordained to reduce her shame, but it didn't work.

Codependency and Enabling

Sexually addicted pastors, like all sex addicts, are codependent. They need a great deal of approval from others because they can't give it to themselves. Sexually addicted pastors might think, "What better place to gain approval from lots of people than in a congregation?"

Once, after giving a lecture on codependency, a retired pastor's wife came to me and said, "What you are calling codependency is what in seminary we were taught as helping others." This woman thought I was advocating selfishness as a healthier posture. However, I was not encouraging selfishness so much as discouraging codependent and enabling behavior. *Enabling* is a word that is also used frequently in the addiction community to describe those who enable a person to continue their addiction unchallenged. An enabler takes care of people to gain or maintain their approval.

In the pastoral role there is plenty of justification for caretaking, for it is part of the job description. Addicted, codependent pastors take care of lots of people, thinking they will be liked and respected. Under the surface, they may resent all they are expected to do and blame the church for too many demands, but they can't say no. If they did, someone might not like them.

Sexually addicted pastors might see aspects of their own woundedness in the person they seek to help. Certain members of their congregations might have similar abusive histories to those of their pastors. Pastors who experience this similarity may overidentify with these members. Caring for these members can be a vicarious way of trying to care for themselves.

Denial

Sex addicts follow the family rule they learned, which is to deny all problems. The problem of denial is especially acute for sexually addicted pastors. For one thing, the consequences of sexual immorality are profound. This creates great fear, and denial can result. What's more, pastors are not supposed to have problems. Church people don't like their pastors to have problems. A sexually addicted pastor might say, "My role says that I need to be perfect. I take care of others. They look to me. People need me to be their spiritual leader, their inspiration. I can't admit to any problems, much less sexual ones."

Rather than ask for help, many pastors go on leading a double life. This is intensely lonely. While they might take great care of their congregations, they do not take care of themselves. They are dying spiritually.

A factor that makes it easy for pastors to deny their problems is that their daily activities are largely unsupervised. Their time is usually their own. They are not accountable to anyone. This free, unsupervised time leaves pastors vulnerable to temptation.

Added to this is the fact that pastors are so esteemed, most people in the congregation are afraid to confront them. A church member might ask, "Who am I to challenge our pastor's behaviors?" This also leaves pastors devoid of real accountability. I have been in churches in which the pastor claimed to have set up personal accountability, but had actually surrounded himself with friends who were all too afraid to really confront him when they sensed something was wrong. In these cases, the whole system of the congregation, along with the pastor, is in denial.

Withdrawal

One characteristic particularly prevalent to sexually addicted clergy is withdrawal, the act of distancing oneself from others. The roles of pastor and priest offer built-in excuses to withdraw. Clergy are supposed to contemplate and meditate. They are expected to have many deep concerns on their mind.

Sexually addicted pastors and priests can escape by working in their studies. As the addiction progresses, they will seem more and more withdrawn. In the height of the disease a normally social pastor may cut off most contact with the outside world. Besides denying their problem, withdrawn sexually addicted pastors and priests will also avoid supervision by mentors, superiors, or other professionals.

It is easy for clergy to say, "I have a meeting downtown, or a hospital call to make, or a sermon to write. I need some time alone in my study. I'm in prayer. Don't bother me." Who would bother such a spiritual person on such spiritual business? It always shocks us later on to find out that this spiritual business might really have been sexual in nature. If pastors seem unable to account for their time, they might be withdrawing. It is the responsibility of the congregation, or its leadership, to require accountability.

Is it intrusive to ask clergy to document their activities? I don't think so. While on the surface they may be angry and defensive, underneath they are ashamed of their double life. A part of them will be grateful to be confronted.

Blackouts

Addicts of all kinds experience blackouts. Sexually addicted pastors and priests may not be able to remember periods of time. Perhaps they will claim to be preoccupied with important matters, even naming it a "spiritual preoccupation." They might also claim to be busy, running from place to place. They might miss appointments or forget important events. If this happens more and more, these are signs the disease is progressing.

Rigidity

Sexually addicted pastors and priests seek many ways to control their disease. They may teach rigid theological formulas or follow certain routines. They may think that if they win enough church members, if the budget is large enough, if they make enough calls, or if they counsel enough, then they will be rewarded with relief from sexual temptations.

This thinking reflects a cycle of guilt in which a pastor tries to expiate sexual sins by doing good works. When more sexual sins take place, more good works need to follow. This cycle of guilt is also a cycle of burnout. In a recent informal survey conducted with twenty-five sexually addicted pastors, 80 percent reported they also suffered from workaholism.

Blaming

Rigidity and denial lead to blaming. Sexually addicted pastors and priests follow another rule they learned in their families, "We don't accept personal responsibility, we blame others." These pastors and priests can point the finger at others and add theological justification for their behavior. They may argue, "How could it be my fault that I sexually acted out? There is so much sexual temptation out there in the world."

The sexually addicted pastor who has exploited a parishioner may use what I call the "Potiphar's Wife Defense." This defense claims that it is always the other person's fault for being so aggressive and demanding. It is not uncommon for sexually addicted clergy to (perhaps unconsciously) pick out others who are needy, aggressive, and demanding. They may also pick out those who have learned that the way they get attention is by being sexual. This could be due to their own experiences of sexual abuse. When publicly exposed, the pastors who do this have the excuse of blaming these "needy and aggressive" people.

Reaction Formation

Rigidity, blaming, and denial also lead to what we call "reaction formation." This behavior involves reacting to phenomena in others that you are concerned about in yourself. A sexually addicted pastor or priest will react to sexual sins "out there" in others and in the world. This reaction reflects the need to control the sexual temptation in others in order to control oneself. Jimmy Swaggart ranted and railed against "prostitutes, pimps, and pornographers" while at the same time being involved with prostitutes. This is reaction formation. Ironically, the hypocrisy of his preaching and his attempts to reveal the sexual sins of other pastors led one pastor to hire a private detective to expose him.

Loss of Personal Values

Sex addicts, particularly as their disease progresses, experience a loss of personal values. This dynamic is particularly striking for pastors and priests who are supposed to be moral people. When they hear of a sexual sin, people often ask, "How could they do such a thing; don't they know any better?" Sexually addicted clergy generally do know better. They are aware of rules, laws, restrictions, and morals. But their addiction is so unmanageable they pursue it anyway. They also tell themselves it is all right to break some of the rules, some of the time. They may argue they aren't hurting their family or congregation by being involved in masturbation or pornography. Even when caught abusing or exploiting a parishioner, they have elaborate justifications about how the sexual activity is part of caring pastoral activity.

Sex Equals Love

Sex equals love is one of the four core beliefs of sex addicts. The only physical nurturing some sex addicts received as children was sexual in nature. Never having experienced healthy touching of any kind, they search desperately for nurturing and begin to equate it with sex.

Because of this core belief, sexually addicted clergy may delude themselves into thinking that since they are caregivers, anything they do—including sexual activity—is caring. Many pastors and priests who are sexual exploiters and abusers have said to me that their victims needed love, understanding, and care. It seemed natural to nurture them, but this nurturing often led to sex.

A pastor might counsel a woman who has a bad marriage. As she tells the details of her lonely life, the pastor really does begin to care for her. He may then say to himself, "I will be the first understanding man

in her life. I will show her what healthy sex with a 'gentle' man is like."
Under this caring delusion, some clergy really do think sex equals love
and is a caring activity.

The Myth of the Perfect Person

The selfishness of sexual exploitation can be an extension of sex
addicts' belief that there is a perfect person out there to nurture them.
For many, sexual addiction is the pursuit of this perfect partner. Having
been abandoned by one or more significant persons in their life, they
seek a perfect person to fill their loneliness.[4] If they are married, they
will have given up on the idea that their spouse is this person, and anger
and frustration result.

A typical congregation is full of such people. They may perceive the
all-wise, all-caring pastor to be such a savior. If they seek to fulfill needs
that their parents left unfilled, they will project on the pastor qualities
of their parents, hoping that the pastor will be a better parent.

Sexually addicted clergy and needy parishioners are mutual elements
in an explosive situation. Parishioners will do anything for the clergy,
even violate moral boundaries. They may imagine themselves to be the
person who will take care of the pastor in ways that others, including
the pastor's spouse, don't. They may also get a sense of power from being
involved with this "saint." Ultimately, of course, the responsibility for
sexual activity rests with the pastor.

Anger

Addicts experience much anger, sometimes unconsciously and sometimes consciously. Usually they don't have the tools to express this in
healthy ways. It is then repressed and becomes a deep and long-lasting
depression, or it may be expressed in indirect and passive ways.

Sexually addicted pastors and priests may allow themselves to feel
abused by their role, feeling their congregations take advantage of them.
One of a sex addict's core beliefs is that "no one takes care of me but
myself." This attitude fuels the sexually addicted pastor's inclination to
take advantage of people who offer them sex.

Sexually addicted pastors may also experience gender hatred. If a pastor is angry at all women, it may be that all women remind him of his abusive mother. Whatever woman is in his office at any particular moment will be in danger of that anger.

It is widely believed that people who abuse and exploit sexually are angry with their victims. It is certainly true that anger, so early developed, can be a part of any act of sexual abuse or exploitation. In helping clergy who commit these sins, we must recognize that their anger at men or women is often the symptom of much deeper, unhealed anger at others who have hurt them.

Entitlement

One reason sex addicts feel they can express anger in any way they see fit is that they believe they deserve to get their needs met. The sense of entitlement is particularly dangerous for sexually addicted clergy. Their role places them in great isolation and at the same time makes many demands on them. As they seek to fulfill these demands, they may also come to believe they deserve to get some rewards. They are lonely and don't know how to reach out to others in healthy ways to meet their needs except through sexual addiction. Perhaps anger allows them to cross definite boundaries. Or perhaps it is their depression, loneliness, or desperation to get some nurturing.

The wife of an evangelist told me about her husband's numerous sexual encounters with women who came to him for counseling after a revival. "I just did a good job. I won a lot of souls for Christ, now I need to take care of myself," he would tell himself. "These women seem so grateful and willing. I am a loving person. They won't be harmed by this, and I am entitled to it."

The Delusion of Special Protection

Sexually addicted clergy are guilty of magical thinking. "If I am good, good will come to me. If I am bad, bad will come to me." Sexually addicted pastors and priests guilty of "bad things" try to cover their sins with more "good things." They continually try to keep a positive balance with God so they won't be punished.

Sexually addicted clergy also have a hope that their ordination makes them special and perhaps protected by God. This delusion can cause them to take great risks that may bring danger to themselves or to others. Risk also brings with it excitement, a high that in itself can be addicting.

In cases of sexual abuse or exploitation, the delusion of sexually addicted clergy is that they won't get caught, that they are specially protected, and that what they are doing is all right because they are ordained. This delusion is very dangerous. It allows sexually addicted clergy to believe that their activity is, in fact, not damaging to their victims. They may even delude themselves into believing, "If I denied myself to them, they would feel abandoned."

Yet sex addicts also, paradoxically, want to be caught. Their disease is unmanageable, and they know they can't stop on their own. Unconsciously, they may slip up and do things that reveal their secret. When they are found out, they may be afraid and ashamed, but they will also be relieved.

Warning Signs

Here are twelve common warning signs that should prompt a congregation or its leadership to investigate questions concerning its clergy. The pastor or priest:

1. **Exhibits symptoms of depression**. The pastor is normally positive or content but now seems depressed or moody.
2. **Has mood swings**. The pastor's moods seem to fluctuate wildly. Sometimes the pastor does a lot of work, at other times no work gets done.
3. **Spends a great deal of time alone**. The pastor always seems to be alone and doesn't like questions regarding this.
4. **Counsels others at strange times and places**. The pastor is seen counseling people late at night, behind closed doors, in restaurants, or in frequent home visits to one particular church member.
5. **Has a troubled marriage.** The spouse seems depressed or angry. Rumors float around about the unhappiness of the marriage.

6. **Uses sexual humor**. This could be a form of sexual exhibitionism and, depending on people's reactions, a form of sexual recruitment.
7. **Touches people often**. Some parishioners are uncomfortable with the pastor's frequent touches or hugs.
8. **Seems lonely.** The pastor may talk about this in superficial ways, not really asking for help, just complaining about needs that are never met.
9. **Preaches about personal issues**. People come out of church feeling sorry for the poor pastor, but no one knows how to help because there hasn't been a direct request.
10. **Uses pornography**. The pastor frequents places where pornography or sexual activity is known to be available, or uses Internet pornography.
11. **Is surrounded by rumors**. Rumors abound regarding the pastor's sexual activities.
12. **Forms "special" relationships with certain types of people**. In the worst-case scenario, this might be children or adolescents.

This is a partial list. Many of these warning signs could point to other kinds of personal trouble besides sexual addiction. However, when you see these warning signs, the responsible thing to do is to ask the pastor what is going on.

When Nathan confronted King David about his adultery, David was publicly humiliated. However, he accepted his sin, confessed it, asked for forgiveness, and accepted the consequences. These signs of David's acceptance of his sinfulness were also signs of his potential for health. I believe Nathan confronted David not to judge him but to restore him to right relationship with God (2 Samuel 12:7).

Thousands of sexually addicted clergy are alone, discouraged, and afraid. Who can they talk to about their problems or their wounds? If we are to heal rather than shoot our wounded, we must understand their problems. And we must follow the example of the prophet Nathan in resolving them.

Sexually addicted pastors can be healed. However, as they themselves know, they have a lifetime disease. If they have exploited or abused parishioners, they should not be restored to their positions, not only to protect the victims, but also to protect the addicts from falling back into addictive behavior.

I know many sexually addicted clergy who have found healing. Humble and penitent about the damage they have done to themselves and others, they are in many ways healthier than some of their colleagues. They have learned from their pain and are stronger and wiser. They have gone from being unhealed wounders to being wounded healers.

Finally, to those pastors who recognize some of their own behaviors, be of good courage. Despite your worst behaviors, there is still the promise of grace. You can stop hurting yourself and others, but only if you reach out for help. May you find the strength to ask for that help now.

CHAPTER 13

HEALING FOR CONGREGATIONS

I know a pastor whose predecessor was accused of having sex with a number of boys from his confirmation class. The new pastor described to me how much pain the congregation experienced because of this abuse. One of the victims even threatened to bomb the church.

In Wisconsin, an adult survivor of sexual abuse by a priest was arrested because he threatened to kill the priest. The man, not the priest, is in jail.

In Minneapolis, one attorney successfully sued pastors and churches for millions of dollars for the sexual damage they caused to child and adult victims.

In another state, a church council member had affairs with fifteen married women in one adult Sunday school class. Husbands are angry. The whole church is in shock. Members don't trust each other. Some are threatening to leave and start a new church.

Meanwhile, tremendous public attention has been focused on several well-known televangelists because of their sexual misconduct.

These are a few examples of the pain and grief that sexual misconduct by a pastor, priest, or church leader can create in the church. This chapter is about how sexual sin and addiction affect congregations and what we might do to heal these situations.

UNHEALTHY CHURCHES

We must begin by accepting the fact that many congregations are very unhealthy themselves. Unhealthy churches are likely to call or hire a pastor, priest, or church leader who is also unhealthy. It is important to understand the dynamics of an unhealthy church so we know the entire picture of where healing needs to take place.

I recently spoke to a female pastor who was directing a conference on clergy sexual misconduct. I asked if there would be workshops on how to get help for such pastors. Surprised at my question, she said the thought of dealing with perpetrators at the conference was enough to raise her blood pressure. After further discussion she said, "I guess we never considered the possibility of putting these pastors back together."

There is tremendous anger in the church about sexual sin. This anger leads to judgmental behavior, blaming, and a great deal of self-righteousness. All of these behaviors illustrate that the church at many levels can demonstrate the same dysfunctional characteristics that families do. Why would that be surprising? People from families go to church and create a church family. As described in chapter 5, that means churches might have unhealthy boundaries, might follow unhealthy rules, members might play unhealthy roles, and various kinds of addictions might be present.

Three of the unhealthy rules are: we don't talk, we don't feel, and we blame others for our problems. In a dysfunctional church, people get together not to share intimate fellowship but because they have anxieties and fears about God and about themselves. They have feelings but since they don't talk about their problems, and since everyone wants to be liked, they blame others for their problems. Silence and blame have the potential to damage others spiritually and emotionally.

I am aware of churches, for example, in which pastors have been sexual with up to sixty people. One such pastor remained in his pulpit for twenty-five years! The victims said nothing, others who knew said nothing, and of course, the pastor said nothing. Imagine the individual and collective pain people endured in that church for twenty-five years. Yet many members of the community thought this pastor was an ideal public figure and that this church was the ideal church.

Dysfunctional churches are not places of healing. If the church is to offer help for sexual addiction, it must begin by talking and feeling. I have often said, the greatest enemy of sexual health is silence.

Traditionally, the church has followed the don't-talk rule, thinking it was the most caring thing to do. It has not wanted to ruin anyone's reputation by making the situation public. Victims, in many cases, have felt ignored. The church has further harmed them by not taking more seriously their problems and long-lasting harm. Recently, many victims have turned to the legal system to make the point of how seriously they have been hurt. Many victims I know are not interested in money from lawsuits; they are interested in justice. Justice means they are heard and that the church takes responsibility for its failure to protect them. I know one victim who had a face-to-face meeting with the bishop of that area. Even though the bishop was not the one who had committed the sexual offense, he apologized to the victim sincerely on behalf of the church. This had a wonderfully healing effect.

Regardless of the legal implications of abuse, the church must grapple openly with the issue of sexual abuse within the church. We can no longer hide behind the no-talk rule. We must do something about the problem.

If we are to heal the wounds of the congregation, we must bring healing to two groups—primary victims and secondary victims. Those who have had direct sexual involvement with pastors or church leaders are primary victims. Those whose trust in the pastor or church leader has been betrayed are secondary victims.

CARING FOR PRIMARY VICTIMS

Primary victims have been sexually harassed, sexually teased, touched inappropriately, told sexual jokes, or had a sexual relationship with pastors or church leaders. As a result, victims are wounded by the sexual activity and need help. There are several actions the church can take.

Provide Advocates

Victims may not recognize they are victims. Just like incest victims or other abuse victims, they may assume responsibility and feel guilty for the sexual activity. They may think it is not that important an event. They may have reasons why they don't want others, including their families, to know about it. In some extremely abusive and painful situations, they may not remember the event.

As victims begin to recognize their pain, they need advocates to help them process their healing. The advocate's job is to assure that the victim is heard and believed, and also to assure the victim gets counseling. The advocate may accompany the victim to meetings with church leaders and help the victim to state the facts. The advocate takes note of the church's response and makes sure the victim understands and hears it. The advocate may help the victim state the need for counseling and for financial assistance in getting it.

An advocate can be a counselor, lawyer, or concerned person. A number of denominations currently have people who function in this role.

Advocates may be the first ones to whom victims reveal details about their abuse. Advocates should be trained in following protective procedures, particularly if the victim is a minor. Victims need to know they are safe and that help is available. They may not have the strength to pursue help on their own.

The most critical element in the process, at least initially, is believing the victim. Although there are cases in which victims are not telling the whole truth, researchers have found that such cases are relatively rare. Remember that what is being told is the victim's perception of the facts. Even if that perception is not entirely accurate, it may be very real to the victim. Victims need to hear that their report and perceptions are accepted and that they will get help.

A church or a denomination needs to investigate all reports of sexual misconduct. While this is going on, they need to keep victims and their advocates informed of the process. Communication needs to be truthful and prompt. Many victims report that their phone calls are not returned or that they are ignored. It will not always be the job of church officials to listen to victims, but they can let them know they understand how hurtful the experience has been.

Being believed allows victims to feel safe. Their hurt has been heard and accepted. By believing victims, the church is saying it takes the situation seriously, it will do something about it, and it will take action to prevent the abuse from happening again.

Being believed may be a new experience for victims. It didn't happen in their families and it hasn't happened much historically. Advocates and others may need to continue to reinforce the fact that victims are believed. Ultimately, the feeling of being believed leads to a sense of peace and perhaps even a sense of justice.

Provide Fellowship

During the initial process of getting help it is very important for the church to offer fellowship to victims. If the facts of the situation are known locally, victims may feel extremely uneasy participating in their local church, and perhaps in any church. The church needs to be considerate of victims, letting them know they are welcome at their own time and comfort level to come back to church, or that the church will help them find another church in which they feel more comfortable.

Provide Counseling

This is perhaps the most important of all initial considerations. Victims, with the help of their advocates, must find counseling support. This can be individual therapy, a counseling group, or both. Some cities have support and counseling groups for victims of pastoral sexual abuse. Many counseling agencies have counselors who specialize in this kind of problem.

Because of the nature of this situation, the counselor should not be a pastoral counselor because there may be too much negative identification with this role. The counselor may also need to be the same sex as the victim.

The church should offer to pay for this counseling even if the victim has insurance or the financial ability to do so. In this way the church says to the victim that it understands and accepts responsibility for the harm done.

In counseling the victim, the counselor should not focus only on the abuse at hand, but also deal with any earlier abuse suffered at the hands of family or church. Counseling that deals only with the current situation keeps the victim stuck in early phases of healing.

At some point in the counseling process, victims need to move from being victims to being "survivors." Survivors are those whose lives are not controlled by or oriented around the pain of the abuse. There are stages to pass through to get to this place.

Victims must acknowledge and accept past and present abuse. Knowledge may come slowly. Memories, perhaps extremely painful, are sometimes not readily available to the conscious mind. Victims who are in therapy may require months, if not years, to recall all events. Acceptance means that what is remembered is accepted as being abusive. Acceptance may require the victim to confront the abuser. If the abuser is no longer around or alive, it may be that just telling others, including those in the church, is confrontation enough.

Anger about the abuse must be constructively expressed. Many victims get stuck in anger, feeling that if they stay angry, they won't be hurt again. However, being angry traps them in the role of a victim.

Survivors know that they have power over their own lives. They have the ability to set boundaries, to say no, and to take care of themselves. Survivors are able to get on with their lives and work on other issues as they need to. Their recovery may take years, but their peace and serenity will grow daily.

Be Willing to Reconcile

Victims of pastoral sexual abuse may need to be outside of the church for a while. Christians need to see this time not as a spiritual failure, but as a time of healing for the victim.

If victims experience the patience of the church, they will want to come back and be reconciled. If they were partially at fault, survivors may want to admit their part in the affair and ask the forgiveness of the church. Or, in rare cases, they may want to confront and forgive their abuser. Any confrontation should be done in the presence of a counselor. I have had the privilege of participating in such confrontations. It was one of the most powerful healing sessions I have ever experienced.

Provide Preventive Education

The whole church needs education about abuse, beginning with the earliest ages in Sunday school. It can be very much like the education we give children about abuse in school. I envision a time when both pastors who have abused and survivors who have been abused can tell their stories to churches. This could be educational in helping people know what dangerous situations to look for and avoid, and how to establish healthy boundaries for themselves. Any education of this kind should include lots of advice about how and where to get help.

CARING FOR SECONDARY VICTIMS

Secondary victims are members of the congregation who placed their spiritual trust and confidence in the pastor or leader. Secondary victims can also be members of the local community who knew the pastor or church leader. The strength of their faith may rest with the witness and example of this pastor. When that is betrayed by inappropriate, sinful sexual activity of any kind, there can be a massive injury to the person's ability to trust anyone, including God.

When the pastor sins sexually, some might tell church members, "Put your faith in God, not in this pastor." Others might say, "Forgive and forget. That is the Christian thing to do." If we are to offer healing from the wounds of sexual misconduct, we must break with tradition. Most of all we must be honest with each other. Strategies to heal the wounds sexual addiction has caused millions of secondary victims in thousands of churches includes breaking the silence, grieving, reconciliation, and prevention.

Breaking the Silence: "We Do Talk, We Don't Deny or Minimize"

I met with a group of people from a church who were extremely angry about the handling of a former pastor's sexual misconduct. The pastor had been abusing young boys, and the leaders of the church who knew of the abuse sent him to treatment without informing the congregation. Later, the pastor went on to a new church without saying goodbye at the old church. Seven years later, one of his victims sued him. Only when the news hit the paper did members of the congregation know what had really happened. Upon hearing the real story, members of this group were furious with the pastor and with church officials who hadn't told them the truth.

In this case, the congregation should have been told because there may have been other abuse victims who needed help. But there are other reasons for breaking the silence. The rumors circulating in this congregation were dividing the congregation. People were taking sides in the debate over what really happened. The congregation was ashamed, thinking it was their fault that the pastor left.

If the truth had been told it would have been shocking and painful. However, all of the things the church tried to avoid eventually happened anyway, with deeper hurt and anger. This congregation was victimized twice, once by their pastor and once by their leaders. By avoiding the consequences, the church prevented both the pastor and the congregation from getting real help.

Here are some steps churches can follow to break the silence.

1. Tell the Truth Immediately

Breaking the silence means telling the truth. The first Sunday after the facts become known and are verified, an appropriate leader must tell the congregation the general nature of the facts. I recommend that a prepared statement be read and distributed to all members, and in some cases the media. The statement should simply outline the facts as they are known and describe the plan for the pastor and church.

2. Encourage Church Members to Talk in Healthy Ways

Members should be encouraged to talk about their feelings of hurt, betrayal, and anger, but they should not gossip about the specific details or speculate about who was involved with the pastor.

3. Conduct Public Meetings

The church should conduct public meetings that allow people to come together and talk about what happened. Members should be informed about what is going to happen to the pastor and later they should be given updates. The pastor should not be allowed to disappear, never to be heard from again. One congregation conducted a series of three public meetings. In the first meeting the church's lawyer came to explain the legal situation as several victims had sued the pastor and the denomination. In the second meeting people broke up into small groups and freely discussed their feelings about the situation. In the final meeting a pastor from the denomination came to hear the feelings of the congregation as expressed by the representatives of these small groups. He then conducted a healing service in the sanctuary of the church.

Not all members of a church will attend such meetings. Some will not want to face the issues. That is certainly their choice. We should never force anyone to talk about feelings. That in itself might be abusive. The public meetings that take place should be elective and not mandatory.

4. Recognize That Some Feelings Will Be Delayed

Some church members will be very angry. This could be extremely divisive to the church. Public meetings should be conducted with very clear boundaries about acceptable language and conduct. These meetings are for people to express their personal feelings, not to blame or judge others. The expression of anger is certainly acceptable, but it must be done constructively.

Other church members will have doubts about their faith as a result of the sexual misconduct of their pastor. We should allow them the freedom to be honest about this. Instead of judging them for their lack of faith, we must remember that Job and many other people of faith in the Bible had struggles and doubts in difficult situations.

Delayed and mixed feelings mean that one meeting at the time of public exposure is not enough. Meetings at regular intervals should be offered to members. In this way they can also be updated about the process of healing for all concerned: pastor, victim(s), and congregation.

5. Find an Interim Pastor Who Is Trained and Willing to Deal with Feelings and Conflict

The pastor who replaces the abusive pastor needs to be prepared for lots of counseling and small group sharing outside of these meetings. This new pastor, who will need the patience of Job, should be a good listener and accept that many congregants' feelings will be difficult to hear.

6. Provide Resource Lists for Victims

Breaking the silence also means that the church provides help for both primary and secondary victims. The church tells people how to obtain counseling, how to contact an advocate, or how to get financial help for recovery.

7. Provide Resources for Victims of Other Perpetrators

Another strong possibility is that there are people in the church who have been victimized by other pastors, by parents, or by others. The sexual misconduct of the current pastor may bring these memories to the surface. Again, counseling resources should be provided.

8. Provide Education about Sexuality and Sexual Addiction

It is important to inform people about the nature of the disease and how it operates. Such information might help people understand the dynamics of the sinful behavior that took place. We must accept that there will be those in the congregation who are hiding their own sexually addicted lives. If we gently educate the congregation about this disease and inform people about the help that is available, this can lead many to healing. I cannot emphasize enough the quality of gentleness. Sex addicts already have felt enough shame to last them several lifetimes. Judging these behaviors harshly will only increase their shame and force them deeper into hiding.

Several churches I have worked with used the crisis as an opportunity to provide workshops for men, women, and couples on sexuality and sexual purity. A number of support groups developed out of these workshops that are helping people with their own sexual health.

9. Hire a Consultant(s)

These steps require that church leadership develop a healing plan for the church. It might be necessary in some situations to bring in outside consultants to help with this plan. Often the emotions of church leaders are so profound, they prevent leaders from making sound and effective decisions. Some denominations provide this kind of consulting. In the cases of independent churches, there are a variety of people who specialize in doing this kind of work. When in doubt, find a local Christian counselor who might be willing to help.

Grieving: "We Do Feel"

A congregation will experience definite stages of grief. I am borrowing a system for understanding grief from Dr. Glen W. Davidson, who years ago studied the process of feelings that mothers who had lost children went through. The four categories he identified apply very well to all grief situations.

1. Shock and Numbness

When a pastor or church leader sins sexually, it is a shock. It is hard to believe. It is difficult to accept. In some cases, the pain may be so intense the mind takes over and shuts down feelings. Without this protective measure the pain might be unbearable.

The danger of this phase is that it appears people are coping "nicely." A congregation that thinks it is holding up courageously does not know what to do with painful feelings when they surface weeks or months later. People might ask themselves, "Does this mean I am not a good Christian?" Not wanting to seem immature, they have a hard time admitting to the feelings. As a result, they bury their feelings only to have them surface, perhaps even years later.

2. Searching and Yearning

Sometimes, when we lose loved ones, we wish they were back. We search for them. We refuse to change anything in their rooms, hoping that by leaving them alone, they might return. In the same way, congregations may search and yearn for their pastor to return. They may be very quick to forgive and want the pastor to stay. They may create elaborate fantasies about how it couldn't have happened.

One pastor of a church had sexual relationships with at least ten young boys. A woman in the church refused to believe it had happened, even though the pastor went to jail. In her eyes the boys, their parents, the media, and the prosecuting attorney were all wrong about the facts. This is searching and yearning for the pastor to return.

This phase can be one of intense anger. When loved ones die, we are sometimes angry they deserted us. Since the pastor is still alive, the anger may get displaced onto various others. Denominational or church leaders may be blamed for taking the pastor away. The media or lawyers are often targets. Certainly, many victims get blamed for "taking the pastor away from us."

3. Disorientation

When we lose loved ones, we don't know what to do without them. They provided many necessary functions. We have all known widows, for example, whose husbands protected them from things such as driving or paying bills. When the husband dies, the widow is unable to do these basic things.

When a pastor leaves, church members may suffer physical and emotional disorientation. The pastor probably provided many physical functions for the church and certainly offered emotional support to many. I once heard a man remark, "He didn't know how much I relied on him to just get through each day."

Beyond this, the pastor's leaving creates a spiritual disorientation. People will not know how to relate to God, how to interpret Scripture, how to lead worship, or how to pray.

Some people may feel angry at this stage, but most will feel anxious. They worry about who will conduct upcoming services, or they feel a deep dread that something terrible might happen. People may simply be afraid to come to church or be more deeply anxious about life in general. They may find themselves irritable about little things that don't seem related to the church or to the pastor.

Anxiety and anger left unexpressed lead to depression. The whole congregation may seem to be down. The mood is low. Worship is not positive. No joy is present. Individual members may be personally depressed. If the loss of the pastor is not recognized as a powerful factor in their lives, church members may become frightened by their depression. It may seem to come from nowhere, with no explanation. They will be baffled and frightened.

4. Reorganization

After church members have moved through the other phases and expressed their hurts, they come to a period of reorganization in which they accept the situation and move on. Reorganization means the congregation finds or accepts a new pastor. New and creative solutions are found for the problems the pastor used to solve.

The stages of grief just described take various lengths of time to work through. The whole process, if accomplished in a healthy way, typically takes a year or two. This sounds like a long time and people may get impatient with it; however, if enough time is not taken, feelings stay buried, fester, and cause anger and resentments later on.

Reconciliation: "We Don't Blame"

A congregation that wants to heal does not allow itself to blame others for the problems in the church. Instead, it offers understanding and help to those most affected by the sexual sins of its pastors and members.

Victims need to feel welcome at church. Victims' families and the pastor's family need to be embraced. Pastors, if they are in recovery and humble, need to be restored to the church. This does not mean pastors should be restored to former duties, but there might be a time and a place when they are allowed to publicly apologize for their behaviors. Their apology might include a humble acceptance of sinful behavior, an admission of wrongdoing, and an acknowledgment of how painful and destructive the behaviors were. This could be healing for the pastor, the church, and any victims.

Reconciliation may need to take place between the church and the pastor's family. Although the family did not cause the problem, their presence in the church may be a painful reminder of the situation. Instead of ignoring the family, the church should be sensitive to their needs. If the pastor and his or her family have left, the family might be invited back at least to say goodbye. This allows everyone to feel a sense of closure.

In my experience, another person who may need reconciliation is the pastor who immediately replaces the one who has left. This pastor, who needs to be an exceptionally strong and mature Christian, will face enormous difficulties and needs much support. The Minneapolis/St. Paul area now has a support group for pastors in these situations. Reconciliation in the church means that the members accept the difficulties the new pastor faces and are willing to support the pastor in every way possible.

Prevention: "We Do Have Boundaries"

Unhealthy boundaries typify an unhealthy congregation. In such congregations, emotional incest, spiritual mind rape, spiritual invasiveness, abandonment, and all other forms of abuse can take place.

A healthy church is one in which boundaries are respected. Members respect themselves and each other. Members take care of themselves and allow others to do the same. Members work to avoid injuring others emotionally, physically, sexually, and spiritually.

Even Jesus established boundaries for himself. He went into the wilderness to be by himself. He got into a boat and went to the other side of the sea when the crowds got too demanding. Rather than chasing after people to get them to believe his message, he told the truth and allowed it to sink in. And he did everything with love.

To begin the process of changing a church from one with unhealthy boundaries to one with healthy boundaries, we must educate the church about boundaries—how they can be invaded and how much damage such invasion can do. Next, church leaders must model healthy boundaries. They should not respond to every demand of the congregation. And they should not take advantage of others. By modeling healthy boundaries, church leaders show the congregation how to care for themselves and others.[1]

Healing the wounds of a congregation affected by sexual sinfulness is a long painful process. In this pain, however, we can be truly vulnerable with each other about our feelings. Vulnerability leads to intimacy and to profound spiritual friendship. In all things, God works for good on behalf of those who love him. This is the hope of salvation for the whole body of Christ.

CONCLUSION

The inevitable final question is, "Can sexual addiction be cured?" The answer depends on how one defines the word *cure*. In the case of sexual addiction, many Christians want the word cure to mean a permanent removal of all disease. They like to think salvation, faith, and prayer eradicate all sexual temptation and the urge to commit sexual sin. Unfortunately, this is like asking God to remove all sexual desire from the human brain or all sexual temptation from the world.

There is no foolproof cure for sexual addiction. Recovering addicts may have stopped acting out, but they know they are always at risk to act out again. Therefore, they must be continually careful about maintaining their program, going to meetings, and avoiding "slippery" places where temptation lurks. There does come a time when it becomes important for a sex addict to ask, "How am I different from a normal person?" Normal people have temptations and sometimes sin. After seventeen years of sobriety from sexual sin, I do feel normal. I also know I can still be tempted and if I were to fall again, I would probably be right back where I left off very quickly.

As a diabetic, I battle a disease that has no cure. I can manage it, live with it, effectively treat all of the symptoms, but I cannot get rid of it. There is no permanent cure for diabetes. The same is true for my sexual addiction: It also has no permanent cure. But the recovery process does offer me, and many others, healing—an ongoing process of improvement. Lives get better, the pain of abuse diminishes, feelings improve, relationships become more intimate, marriages get stronger, and sexual temptation decreases. This is a healing process, but it is not a cure.

Like the apostle Paul, sex addicts must deal with their "thorn in the flesh":

> To keep me from becoming conceited because of these surpassingly great revelations, there was given me a thorn in my flesh, a messenger of Satan, to torment me. Three times I pleaded with the Lord to take it away from me. But he said to me, "My grace is sufficient for you, for my power is made perfect in weakness." Therefore I will boast all the more gladly about my weaknesses, so that Christ's power may rest on me. That is why, for Christ's sake, I delight in weaknesses, in insults, in hardships, in persecutions, in difficulties. For when I am weak, then I am strong.
>
> 2 CORINTHIANS 12:7–10

Sex addicts, spouses, family members, and others are capable of great spiritual healing, of profound relationships with God, even though their sexual addiction may not be cured. Accepting powerlessness over their disease leaves them with a great humility and need for God, which is a deep aspect of their spiritual healing. Like Paul, their ongoing "thorn in the flesh" allows them to point to their weakness as individuals and to their need for salvation from God.

Ultimately, if all things are possible with God, we can accept that there are sex addicts who may be cured. For them, sexual temptation may never again be a problem. For most, however, this won't happen. Yet, even in the lack of cure there can be great spiritual healing, healing that can be a wonderful witness to the entire Christian community.

This book has been written not to be the final answer to the problem of sexual addiction, but rather to provide information to educate the church. Education gets people talking, and educated talking starts the process of healing.

There is an old Alcoholics Anonymous expression that is used at the end of meetings: "Take what you like and leave the rest." In the course of this book, you may have disagreed with several things you read. Yet it is my hope that you will take what this book has to offer and, even though you may disagree with certain points, use it to stimulate think-ing, prayer, and action. If you are hurting as a result of sexual addiction, don't try to process the hurt yourself. Talk to someone, get some help, work together with others. While sexual sin is devastating, there is hope for healing.

When Jesus became a man, he suffered our fate as human beings. He was humiliated, tortured, and killed. Paul writes that Jesus, "being found in appearance as a man . . . humbled himself and became obedient to death" (Philippians 2:8). Sex addicts also must be obedient unto death—death of their old addictive lifestyles.

Yet Jesus, after dying, rose again. After dying to themselves, sex addicts also can live again. They can experience freedom, spiritual res-urrection, and peace. When they allow Jesus to step into the deepest shadows of their most secret sins, he floods those places with redeeming light.

I wish I could describe to you the testimony of hundreds of sex addicts who have gone through this process of death and rebirth. Lives have been restored, marriages healed, and families strengthened. Careers and economic situations have been rebuilt. Best of all, the recovering sex addict experiences a deep sense of the presence and redeeming grace of God.

There is hope for the sex addict. Over the last seventeen years I have seen hundreds of addicts, spouses, and marriages find that hope and begin the healing journey. If you are one, my prayer is that you will find this hope. You have been wounded and lonely all your life. You don't have to stay that way. There is peace. May you find that peace now.

NOTES

There Is Hope

1. For more information about female sexual addiction, see *No Stones: Women Released from Sexual Shame* by Marnie C. Feree.

Chapter 2. Building-Block Behaviors of Sex Addicts

1. Al Cooper, David Delmonico, and Ron Berg, "Cybersex Users, Abusers, and Compulsives: New Findings and Implications," *Sexual Addiction and Compulsivity* 7, nos. 1 and 2 (2000).

2. The Faithful and True Ministries' website, www.faithfulandtrueministries.com, features numerous articles, including one devoted to masturbation.

Chapter 3. Types of Sexual Addiction

1. Gerald Blanchard, *Sex Offender Treatment: A Psychoeducational Model* (Golden Valley, MN: Institute for Behavioral Medicine, 1988).

Chapter 4. Understanding and Identifying the Characteristics of Sexual Addiction

1. Patrick Carnes, *Don't Call It Love* (New York: Bantam, 1991).

2. Ibid.

3. Craig Nakken, *The Addictive Personality* (Center City, MN: Hazelden, 1988).

4. Developments in the field of psychiatry change so rapidly it is difficult for any writing to keep up with advances being made. New abilities to actually see the brain through the use of diagnostic imaging, like Functional MRI, are literally rewriting the ways in which we have understood the brain.

Chapter 5. Unhealthy Family Dynamics

1. John and Linda Friel, *The Secrets of Dysfunctional Families* (Deerfield Beach, FL: Health Communications, Inc., 1988).

Chapter 6. Family Abuse

1. Patrick Carnes, *Don't Call It Love* (New York: Bantam, 1991).

2. Patricia Love, *The Emotional Incest Syndrome* (New York: Bantam, 1990).

3. Carnes, *Don't Call It Love*.

4. John Bradshaw, *Healing the Shame that Binds You* (Deerfield Beach, FL: Health Communications, Inc., 1988).

5. Sandra Wilson, *Released from Shame* (Downers Grove, IL: InterVarsity, 1990).

6. Patrick Carnes, *Out of the Shadows* (Minneapolis: CompCare, 1983).

Chapter 7. How Sex Addicts Cope with Abuse

1. Harvey Milkman and Stanley Sunderwirth, *Craving for Ecstasy* (Lexington, MA: D.C. Health, 1987).

2. Patrick Carnes, *Don't Call It Love* (New York: Bantam, 1991).

Chapter 10. Treatment Issues in Sexual Addiction

1. The SAST is available on a number of websites, including www.bethesda-workshops.org. The SAI must be ordered directly from its current publisher, The Gentle Path Press.

2. Faithful and True Ministries is working to establish a certified training program for counselors who want to specialize in sex addiction therapy. For more information about training and certification of counselors, consult our website, www.faithfulandtrueministries.com.

3. For more information on these workshops, visit www.bethesdaworkshops.org. Additional websites are listed on pages 228–33 in the Resources section.

4. Read Matthew 11: 28–30.

5. There are many books and resources available to help readers develop a vision. I especially recommend Rick Warren's *The Purpose-Driven Life* (Grand Rapids: Zondervan, 2001).

Chapter 11. Healing for Couples

1. See page 233 in the Resources section for information on support groups for couples.

2. Patrick Carnes, *Don't Call It Love* (New York: Bantam, 1991).

Chapter 12. Sexually Addicted Pastors and Priests

1. The ideas in this chapter were originally published in my article, "Sexual Addiction and Clergy," *Pastoral Psychology* 39, no. 4 (March 1991): 213–35.

2. "How Common Is Pastoral Indiscretion?" *Leadership* 11, no. 1 (Winter 1988): 12–13.

3. Tim LaHaye, *If Ministers Fall, Can They Be Restored?* (Grand Rapids: Zondervan, 1990).

4. Peter Rutter, *Sex in the Forbidden Zone* (Los Angeles: Jeremy P. Tarcher, 1989).

Chapter 13. Healing for Congregations

1. For additional information about boundaries and other topics in this chapter, see Mark Laaser and Nancy Hopkins, eds., *Restoring the Soul of a Church* (Collegeville, MN: Liturgical Press, 1996).

Resources

The following resources are not exhaustive. I provide them as starting points to find help. Once you have decided to get help, you have overcome a major obstacle: You have decided that you can't do it alone and that you need God's help. Contact any of the following organizations and don't be afraid to try more than one place until you find the help you need and feel comfortable with.

ORGANIZATIONS

Faithful and True Ministries

15798 Venture Lane
Eden Prairie, MN 55344
(952) 746-3880
www.faithfulandtrueministries.com

Ministry for sexual wholeness that offers counseling, consulting, workshop ministries, speakers, and published resources.

L.I.F.E. Ministries

P.O. Box 952317
Lake Mary, FL 32795
(407) 647-9560
www.freedomeveryday.org

Support group ministry for sex addicts and co-addicts; provides workbooks and support group materials.

National Association for Christian Recovery

P.O. Box 215
Brea, CA 92822
(714) 529-6227
www.nacronline.com

Organization for recovering persons, including online support groups, suggested resources, and conferences.

Prodigals International

17530 NE Union Hill Road, Suite 160
Redmond, WA 98052
Toll-free (888) 535-5565 or (425) 869-6468
www.iprodigals.com

Christian organization that provides information, support group materials, and assistance for sexual addiction and sexual co-addiction.

National Coalition for the Protection of Children and Families

800 Compton Road, Suite 9224
Cincinnati, OH 45231
HelpLine (800) 583-2964 or (513) 521-6227
www.nationalcoalition.org

Christian organization that provides help and referrals for people struggling with pornography or those interested in fighting pornography.

American Association of Christian Counselors

P.O. Box 739
Forest, VA 24551
Toll-free (800) 526-8673
www.aacc.net

Christian organization for counselors, pastors, and lay leaders; provides lists of counselors professional conferences, and resources including videotapes, audiotapes, books, and other printed materials.

The Society for the Advancement of Sexual Health (SASH)

SASH/The National Office
P.O. Box 725544
Atlanta, GA 31139
(770) 541-9912
www.SASH.org

Secular organization for professionals working with sexual addiction and/or sexual trauma; provides information, resources, and lists of counselors.

Pine Grove Hospital

Gentle Path Program
(888) 574-4673

KeyStone Center Extended Care Unit

2000 Providence Avenue
Chester, PA 19013
Toll-free (800) 733-6840 or (610) 876-8448
www.keystonecenterecu.net

Residential treatment center for healing from sexual compulsivity and trauma.

TWELVE-STEP GROUPS FOR ADDICTS

Each of these fellowships may have meetings in your area. Call to receive meeting information or to find contacts in your area. Each fellowship varies slightly in meeting format or philosophy. One main difference might be how sobriety is defined. For example, Sexaholics Anonymous (SA) has, at least historically, had the strictest definition and the one that Christians would be most comfortable with. SA says that sobriety is sexual abstinence from any sexual activity except with one's spouse. However, even these distinctions might vary from town to town, as each meeting is an autonomous local fellowship. Be aware that telephone numbers and addresses change over time. Be persistent in getting the information you need.

Sexaholics Anonymous (SA)

P.O. Box 11910
Nashville, TN 37222-1910
(615) 331-6230
www.sa.org

Sex Addicts Anonymous (SAA)

P.O. Box 70949
Houston, TX 77270
(713) 869-4902
www.sexaa.org

Sex and Love Addicts Anonymous (SLAA)

P.O. Box 338
Norwood, MA 02062-0338
(781) 255-8825
www.slaafws.org

Alcoholics Anonymous (AA)

AA World Services, Inc.
P.O. Box 459
Grand Central Station
New York, NY 10163
(212) 870-3400
www.alcoholics-anonymous.org

CHRISTIAN SUPPORT GROUPS

Over the years I have seen many ministries establish support groups that in some ways follow the principles of the Twelve Steps, but which also honor Christ as the center of healing. Some may be found through the organizations and websites listed above. I have had the privilege of writing the materials for one, L.I.F.E. (Living In Freedom Everyday) Ministries. They have developed materials for male sex addicts, female sex addicts, spouses, couples, and teens. Their contact information is:

L.I.F.E. Ministries

P.O. Box 952317
Lake Mary, FL 32795
(407) 647-9560

For Co-Addicts

S-Anon International Family Groups (S-Anon)

P.O. Box 111242
Nashville, TN 37222-1242
(615) 833-3152
www.sanon.org

Codependents of Sex Addicts (COSA)

P.O. Box 14537
Minneapolis, MN 55414
(763) 537-6904
www.cosa-recovery.org

Al-Anon

Al-Anon Family Group Headquarters, Inc.
1600 Corporate Landing Parkway
Virginia Beach, VA 23454-5617
(888) 425-2666
www.al-anon.org

Codependents Anonymous (CODA)

P.O. Box 33577
Phoenix, AZ 85067-3577
(602) 277-7991
www.codependents.org

For Couples

Recovering Couples Anonymous (RCA)

P.O. Box 11029
Oakland, CA 94611
(510) 663-2312
www.recovering-couples.org

For Trauma Survivors

Survivors of Incest Anonymous (SIA)

World Service Office
P.O. Box 190
Benson, MD 21018
(410) 893-3322
www.siawso.org

Incest Survivors Anonymous (ISA)

P.O. Box 17245
Long Beach, CA 90807
(562) 428-5599

Adult Children of Alcoholics

World Service Organization, Inc.
P.O. Box 3216
Torrance, CA 90510
(310) 534-1815
www.adultchildren.org

COUNSELING

Having a therapist who is knowledgeable about sexual addiction is critical. However, finding one may be difficult. A Christian counselor trained in sexual addiction is the ideal choice, but unfortunately, such professionals are quite rare. Because more resources are available to provide spiritual support, look first for a clinician who understands sexual addiction. If that person is also a Christian, that's a plus. No ethical counselor will do anything to challenge your faith, and someone who doesn't understand sexual addiction can do more harm than good. Here are some suggestions about how to find a counselor:

1. Ask other recovering people for recommendations.
2. Ask other mental health professionals for counselors trained in addictions.
3. Contact your local drug and alcohol council for referrals.
4. Check the listing of therapists who are members of the National Council on Sexual Addiction and Compulsivity (www.ncsac.org).
5. For specifically Christian resources, check the listing of therapists who are members of an organization like the American Association of Christian Counselors (www.aacc.net). (Understand that this is a general listing and includes pastors and lay people, not just professional therapists.) Even if a person has clinical training, an AACC member may not be familiar with sexual addiction.

It's wise to interview therapists to see if they seem to be an appropriate choice. Here are some questions to ask:

1. Are you trained in treating addictions?
2. Are you specifically familiar with sexual addiction?
3. Have you heard of Dr. Patrick Carnes?
4. Do you recommend the Twelve-Step program of recovery?
5. Do you work from a trauma-based model in treating addictions?
6. How many sexually addicted clients have you treated?
7. What's your definition of sexual sobriety?
8. What's your experience in helping sexual co-addicts?
9. What about couples? How do you work with them?

Professionals can have a variety of educational backgrounds and practice emphases. Below is a brief synopsis of the more common ones.

Education

Be sure to ask what field is represented by the degree. For example, some may have a Ph.D. in history and refer to themselves as "Dr." but that title and degree has nothing to do with qualifications to practice psychotherapy.

Doctoral Degree

These clinicians have achieved the most advanced level of education available, which is usually signified by the initials Ph.D., Ed.D., or PsyD.

Master's Degree

These clinicians have completed a graduate degree, usually identified as a M.A., M.S., or M.F.T.

Type of Counselor

Psychiatrist

This person is a medical doctor who has completed advanced training in mental and emotional disorders. A psychiatrist may prescribe medication and is typically more focused on managing medication than on providing talk therapy.

Psychologist

This person has a doctoral degree but isn't medically trained. He or she may be specifically trained in testing but will also conduct traditional therapy.

Licensed Professional

These clinicians have at least a master's degree and have completed supervision requirements for licensure in their field. Different types include:

Licensed Marriage and Family Therapist

These individuals are specifically trained in marriage and family therapy; they view individuals in the context of their relationships.

Licensed Professional Counselor

These people have met their states' requirement to be licensed as a counselor. They can be at either a master's degree or Ph.D. level. This involved taking a licensure exam and demonstrating a certain amount of supervised counseling hours.

Licensed Clinical Social Worker

Similarly, these people have met either state or national standards to be licensed as social workers. They can specialize in a variety of mental health areas, including marriage and family counseling. Therefore, a license in this field can mean a variety of areas of competence. One should always be careful to investigate what areas of expertise the LCSW is competent in, such as addiction.

Licensed Pastoral Counselor

These counselors have met the requirements of one of several pastoral counseling organizations, involving varying amounts of education, training, and supervision. This is not the same as a state licensure but does constitute demonstrated proficiency in pastoral counseling. Many of these organizations provide training in areas of marriage and family counseling that would be similar to those of an LPC or an LCSW.

Unlicensed Counselor

This person is either a trained counselor who for whatever reason hasn't completed the requirements for licensure, or a lay counselor or minister who doesn't have professional clinical training.

RECOMMENDED READING

Sexual Addiction

Carnes, Patrick. *Contrary to Love*. Minneapolis: CompCare, 1989.

―――. *Don't Call It Love*. New York: Bantam Books, 1991.

―――. *Facing the Shadow: Starting Sexual and Relationship Recovery*. Wickenburg, AZ: Gentle Path, 2001.

―――. *Out of the Shadows*. Minneapolis: CompCare, 1992.

―――. *Sexual Anorexia*. Center City, MN: Hazelden, 1997.

Earle, Ralph, and Gregory Crow. *Lonely All the Time*. New York: Pocket, 1989.

Earle, Ralph, and Mark Laaser. *Pornography Trap*. Kansas City: Beacon Hill, 2002.

Ferree, Marnie C. *A L.I.F.E. Guide: Women Living in Freedom Everyday*. Fairfax, VA: Xulon, 2002.

―――. *No Stones: Women Redeemed from Sexual Shame*. Fairfax, VA: Xulon, 2002.

Laaser, Mark. *A L.I.F.E. Guide: Men Living in Freedom Everyday*. Fairfax, VA: Xulon, 2002.

―――. *Faithful and True Workbook*. Nashville: Lifeway, 1996.

Means, Patrick. *Men's Secret Wars*. Grand Rapids: Revell, 1996.

Melody, Pia. *Facing Love Addiction*. San Francisco: Harper, 1992.

Willingham, Russell, and Bob Davies. *Breaking Free: Understanding Sexual Addiction and the Healing Power of Jesus*. Downers Grove, IL: Inter-Varsity, 1999.

Young, Kimberly S. *Caught in the Net: How to Recognize the Signs of Internet Addiction*. New York: John Wiley, 1998.

Coaddiction/Codependency

Beattie, Melody. *Beyond Codependency*. New York: Harper/Hazelden, 1989.

―――. *Codependent No More*. New York: Harper/Hazelden, 1987.

Hemfelt, Robert, Frank Minirith, and Paul Meir. *Love Is a Choice*. Nashville: Nelson, 1989.

Means, Marsha. *Living with Your Husband's Secret Wars*, Grand Rapid: Revell, 1999.

―――. *Partner's Healing Journey Workbook*. Redmond, WA: Prodigals International, 2001.

Norwood, Robin. *Women Who Love Too Much*. New York: Pocket, 1991.

Schneider, Jennifer. *Back from Betrayal*. Tucson: Recovery Resources, 2001.

Whitfield, Charles L. *Boundaries and Relationships*. Deerfield Beach, FL: Health Communications, 1993.

Sexual Abuse

Adams, Kenneth M. *Silently Seduced: Understanding Covert Incest*. Deerfield Beach, FL: Health Communications, 1991.

Allender, Dan B. *The Wounded Heart*. Colorado Springs: NavPress, 1990.

Bass, Ellen, and Laura Davis. *Courage to Heal*. New York: Harper and Row, 1988.

Blume, E. Sue. *Secret Survivors*. New York: Ballantine, 1991.

Engel, Beverly. *Partners in Recovery*. Los Angeles: Lowell, 1991.

Friberg, Nils C., and Mark Laaser. *Before the Fall: Preventing Pastoral Sexual Abuse*. Collegeville, MN: Liturgical Press, 1998.

Hopkins, Nancy Myer, and Mark Laaser, eds. *Restoring the Soul of a Church: Healing Congregations Wounded by Clergy Sexual Misconduct*. Collegeville, MN: Liturgical Press, 1995.

Hunter, Mic. *Abused Boys: The Neglected Victims of Sexual Abuse*. New York: Fawcett, 1991.

Langberg, Diane. *On the Threshold of Hope*. Wheaton, IL: Tyndale, 1999.

Lew, Mike. *Victims No Longer: Men Recovering from Incest and Other Sexual Child Abuse*. New York: Harper and Row, 1990.

Love, Patricia. *Emotional Incest Syndrome*. New York: Bantam, 1990.

Murray, Marilyn. *Prisoner of Another War*. Berkeley, CA: PageMill, 1991.

Family-of-Origin Issues

Black, Claudia. *It Will Never Happen to Me*. Denver: M.A.C. Publications, 1982.

Bradshaw, John. *Healing the Shame that Binds You*. Deerfield Beach, FL: Health Communications, 1988.

———. *Homecoming*. New York: Bantam, 1990.

Dayton, Tian. *Trauma and Addiction*. Deerfield Beach, FL: Health Communications, 2000.

Friel, John, and Linda Friel. *Adult Children: The Secrets of Dysfunctional Families*. Deerfield Beach, FL: Health Communications, 1988.

Hemfelt, Robert, and Paul Warren. *Kids Who Carry Our Pain*. Nashville: Nelson, 1990.

Sanford, Linda T. *Strong at the Broken Places*. New York: Avon, 1990.

Smalley, Gary, and John Trent. *The Blessing Workbook*. Nashville: Nelson, 1993.

Whitfield, Charles. *Healing the Child Within*. Deerfield Beach, FL: Health Communications, 1987.

Couples Recovery

Beam, Joe. *Forgiven Forever*. West Monroe, LA: Howard, 1998.

Carder, Dave. *Torn Asunder: Recovering from Extramarital Affairs*. Chicago: Moody, 1991.

———. *Torn Asunder Workbook*. Chicago: Moody, 2001.

Carnes, Patrick, Debra Laaser, and Mark Laaser. *Open Hearts: Renewing Relationships with Recovery, Romance and Reality*. Wickenburg, AZ: Gentle Path, 1999.

Clinton, Tim. *Before a Bad Goodbye*. Nashville: Word, 1999.

Harvey, Donald. *I Love You—Talk to Me*. Grand Rapids: Baker, 1996.

Rainey, Dennis, and Barbara Rainey. *Moments Together for Couples: Devotions for Drawing Near to God and One Another*. Ventura, CA: Regal, 1995.

Healthy Sexuality

Hart, Archibald. *The Sexual Man*. Dallas: Word, 1994.

Hart, Archibald, Catherine Hart Weber, and Debra Taylor. *Secrets of Eve*. Nashville: Word, 1998.

Laaser, Mark. *Talking to Your Kids about Sex*. Colorado Springs: WaterBrook, 1999.

Maltz, Wendy. *Sexual Healing Journey*. New York: Harper Perennial, 1992.

Penner, Cliff, and Joyce Penner. *Restoring the Pleasure*. Dallas: Word, 1993.

Rosenau, Doug. *The Celebration of Sex*. Nashville: Nelson, 1994.

General Recovery

Amen, Daniel. *Change Your Brain, Change Your Life*. New York: Times, 1998.

Burns, David. *Feeling Good: The New Mood Therapy*. New York: Avon, 1980.

Carnes, Patrick. *Gentle Path Through the Twelve Steps*. Center City, MN: Hazelden, 1993.

Cloud, Henry, and John Townsend. *Boundaries*. Grand Rapids: Zondervan, 1992.

———. *Safe People*. Grand Rapids: Zondervan, 1995.

Dodd, Chip. *The Voice of the Heart*. Franklin, TN: Sage Hill, 2001.

May, Gerald. *Addiction and Grace*. New York: Harper, 1988.

Milkman, Harvey, and Stanley Sunderwirth. *Craving for Ecstasy: The Consciousness and Chemistry of Escape*. Lexington, MA: Lexington, 1987.

Peck, M. Scott. *The Road Less Traveled*. New York: Simon and Schuster, 1978.

Sexaholics Anonymous. Simi Valley, CA: SA Literature, 1989.

Stoop, David. *Real Solutions for Forgiving the Unforgivable*. Ann Arbor, MI: Servant, 2001.

Wilson, Sandra. *Released from Shame: Recovery for Adult Children of Dysfunctional Families*. Downers Grove, IL: InterVarsity, 1990.

Bibles

Clinton, Tim, Edward Hindson, and George Ohlschlager, eds. *The Soul Care Bible* (New King James Version). Nashville: Nelson, 2001.

Hemfelt, Robert, and Richard Fowler, *Serenity: A Companion for Twelve-Step Recovery*. Nashville: Nelson, 1990.

Peterson, Eugene H. *The Message*. Colorado Springs: NavPress, 1994.

Recovery Devotional Bible (New International Version). Grand Rapids: Zondervan, 1993.

Inspirational Reading

Answers in the Heart: Daily Meditations for Men and Women Recovering from Sex Addiction. San Francisco: Harper/Hazelden, 1989.

The Bible Promise Book (New International Version). Uhrichsville, OH: Barbour, 1990.

Chambers, Oswald. *My Utmost for His Highest*. Uhrichsville, OH: Barbour, 1963.

Crabb, Larry. *Inside Out*. Colorado Springs: NavPress, 1988.

———. *Shattered Dreams: God's Unexpected Pathway to Joy*. Colorado Springs: WaterBrook, 2001.

Hurnard, Hannah. *Hinds' Feet on High Places*. Wheaton, IL: Living, 1975.

Lucado, Max. *In the Grip of Grace*. Nashville: Word, 1996.

———. *You Are Special*. Wheaton, IL: Crossway, 1997.

Moore, Beth. *Breaking Free*. Nashville: Broadman and Holman, 2000.

———. *Breaking Free Workbook*. Nashville: LifeWay, 1999.

Nouwen, Henri. *The Inner Voice of Love: A Journey Through Anguish to Freedom*. New York: Image, 1996.

———. *Life of the Beloved*. New York: Crossroad, 1992.

Rivers, Francine. *Redeeming Love*. Chicago: Multnomah, 1997.

Wilson, Sandra D. *Into Abba's Arms: Finding the Acceptance You've Always Wanted*. Wheaton, IL: Tyndale, 1998.